To Maria and Je... Love, Gerry

ENEMIES AND HOW TO LOVE THEM

Gerard A. Vanderhaar

ENEMIES
and how to love them

TWENTY-THIRD PUBLICATIONS
Mystic, Connecticut

Library of Congress Catalog Card Number 85-50061

ISBN 0-89622-241-1

Edited by Alice Fleming
Designed by John G. van Bemmel
Cover design by Kathy Michalove

IN GRATITUDE

to Bishop Carroll Dozier, who encouraged me from the beginning;

to Sister Chris Dobrowolski, I.H.M., Rev. Pat Driskell, and Sister Ginny King, O.P., of the Mid-South Peace and Justice Center, for their help and inspiration;

to Robert Rhode, author and friend, who pointed out the significance of the War and Peace Myths, and who shared his realistic insights into the pitfalls of publishing;

to my colleagues in the Humanities Department of Christian Brothers College for their support;

to the National Council and National Coordinators of Pax Christi USA, for their expressions of confidence;

to Etienne De Jonghe, International Secretary of Pax Christi, for arranging my visit to Moscow to meet with representatives of the Russian Orthodox Church in 1980;

to my wife Janice, above all, for her patience, encouragement and timely advice, and for being there to pick up the pieces when I finished.

CONTENTS

INTRODUCTION

In a haunting scene in the short 1963 Polish film "The Magician," a man in a vague military uniform attracts a half dozen young boys to line up with toy popguns. He marches them to a carnival booth where pretty dolls are arrayed on shelves, and orders them to shoot. When the boys are reluctant, the word "enemy" flashes on the screen over the dolls. The word has a magical effect. The boys draw themselves up, aim their guns, and smash the dolls.

"Enemy" is a powerful image. When I perceive another person as enemy, my first reaction is fear and hostility. Putting the label "enemy" on others provokes considerable aggressive behavior. A high school football coach identified the players on the other side as enemies. "The object on every play is to hit your man so hard he won't get up afterwards." President Richard Nixon once said, as though it were a perfectly natural attitude, "I reward my friends and punish my enemies." His staff drew up an Enemies List, then used what they called dirty tricks against people identified as opponents of his

Administration. Many Americans oppose Castro's Cuba and Sandinista Nicaragua as enemies of the United States.

The problem of enemies is especially acute in the nuclear age, when the survival of the human race is at stake. The United States has weapons of immense destruction aimed at the nation we consider our enemy. They have equally awesome weapons trained on us.

The ominous forerunner of our nuclear terror is the holocaust perpetrated by Nazi Germany, in which six million Jewish men, women, and children perished. Two elements of that tragedy stand out: the technological ability for wholesale killing, and the ideology of anti-Semitism. When the ideology fueled the technology, the slaughter began. The nuclear threat features an advanced technology, a fearfully expanded ability to exterminate. But the ideology is different. In the nuclear holocaust it will be "the enemy" that prompts us to push the button.

The problem in the Nazi era was not really Hitler. Psychotic personalities often surface in power circles. The problem was much more the millions of people who followed Hitler, who accepted his fascism, who were infected with the disease of anti-Semitism. The surest way of preventing the Nazi holocaust would have been to eliminate the anti-Semitic prejudice in the multitudes who cooperated with the process. The surest way of preventing a nuclear holocaust is to eliminate the enemy prejudice in the citizens of nuclear nations today.

Those of us who take the Christian tradition seriously know that Jesus' answer to the problem of enemies was to love them. At first glance, in a world of international hardball, love of enemies sounds like an oxymoron, a foolish phrase. It smacks of romantic naivete; dangerous because unrealistic. But Jesus' age-old advice might just be the clue that solves the nuclear mystery. Love of enemies deserves a fresh hearing in the context of today's realities.

Religious leaders have called for a new attitude in the face of the nuclear threat. The Catholic bishops at Vatican II, after reviewing the immensely destructive power of the then available weapons, said: "These considerations compel us to undertake an evaluation of war with an entirely new attitude."

Pope John Paul II, during his visit to Hiroshima in 1981, warned that humanity must make "a moral about-face" to prevent annihilation. The U.S. Catholic bishops, in their 1983 Pastoral Letter, *The Challenge of Peace*, wrote: "A refusal (to legitimate nuclear war) will require not only new ideas and new vision, but what the gospel calls conversion of the heart."

Albert Einstein had proclaimed prophetically at the dawn of the nuclear age: "The unleashed power of the atom has changed everything save our mode of thinking, and thus we drift toward unparalleled catastrophe." I believe that love of our enemy, "enemy love," is at the heart of the new mode of thinking, the new vision, the moral about-face so necessary if we are to move beyond the nuclear threat.

But we want to be practical about it. While we may admire the total obedience of an Abraham ordered to sacrifice his son, most of us in our secret hearts would like some assurance that the new way works before we take the leap into it. So, while this book aims at conversion of attitude toward those enemies who threaten us with nuclear annihilation, it concentrates also on enemies closer to home. If we can bring ourselves to love those enemies, and see that love works to reduce the hostility, then we can have greater confidence in championing an effective love toward our nuclear enemies.

The love we are talking about here is not a sentimental journey. It is not necessarily feeling good about our enemies. It is rather a purposeful, firm decision to respect them as human beings, to work hard with them to resolve our differences through the long process of hammering it out. The goal of enemy love is finally to become cooperators in a common effort to improve things for all of us.

The twentieth century's two great prophets of nonviolence, Mohandas Gandhi and Martin Luther King, Jr., opened up a whole range of possibilities for calm, courageous, and effective action to lower the intensity of hostility and resolve it for the good of all concerned. Enemy love makes practical sense when spelled out in a step by step approach based on the experience of nonviolence. It worked for Gandhi in the liberation of India. It worked for King in the civil rights movement. It can work for each of us in meeting the enemies who emerge in our own lives. And it can work in the big picture toward those enemies who hold the nuclear sword over our planet earth.

If it really does work, the practical minded among us might be emboldened to take the leap of faith toward the new attitude, the moral about-face, the conversion of mind and heart that will transform our lives. We will then join the millions of other men and women around the world who are choosing life over death, hope over despair, and reconciliation over conquest.

The first step in exploring enemy love is to take a hard look at enemies. What exactly is an enemy? How do enemies happen? This we will do in chapter one, "The Making of Enemies." Throughout our lives we experience an intricate interaction between our life energy and the cultural forces surrounding us. What we are at any particular time is the result both of our own unique characteristics and those processes that affect us from outside. The second chapter, "Two Myths, Two Mentalities," examines some of the cultural forces that have shaped our approach to enemies.

Because Jesus was the one who gave us the formula of enemy love, it helps to see how he and his earliest followers actually lived it. We will do this in the third chapter, "Jesus and His Enemies." Chapter Four, "Making Sense of Enemy Love," applies the nuts and bolts of nonviolence. The last chapter grapples with the nagging question, "But What About the Russians?" Will enemy love work toward them? We know it has to if our world is to survive. We need to understand who they are and what they've been doing over there for the last eight decades. Finally, an epilogue ties the book together and points out the direction our personal futures should take.

If enough of us see the effectiveness of a genuinely loving approach to enemies, we can move the international process beyond a preoccupation with limited national security, and toward the realization of genuine, global security for everyone.

CHAPTER ONE

THE MAKING
OF ENEMIES

When we begin to explore the meaning of "enemy" we find a wide diversity of characters. Enemies, it seems, come in all styles. To a British soldier on duty in Belfast, they are Irish Republican Army fighters who might ambush him at any time. To a rural peasant in Guatemala, they are expressionless soldiers who roar into the village in a dark green truck. A Palestinian student in Ramallah looks on Israeli settlers in white compounds on the hills as enemies. To a Jewish citizen of Israel, enemies are Arab terrorists who open fire on a crowded Jerusalem street. A century ago many native Americans saw the encroaching white settler as their enemy. To the stalwart pioneers on the frontier, the marauding Indians were enemies.

5

Today we might picture a stolid Soviet fighter pilot or a grim Politburo member as enemies, the same way another generation saw a Nazi storm trooper or a Japanese prime minister.

Our English word "enemy," with all its unpleasant overtones of violence and fear, comes from the Latin *inimicus*, unfriendly. "Adversary," a synonym, implies direct and forceful opposition. An enemy is antagonistic, has a deep-seated dislike, is unfriendly to the point of wanting, as the *Oxford English Dictionary* puts it, to "do ill" to another. We understand an enemy to be someone who actively opposes to the extent of wanting to harm us.

Those who try to outsmart us in a business deal—which may hurt only our pocketbooks—or defeat us in an athletic contest—which may hurt only our pride—we more properly call "opponents" or "antagonists," or perhaps "rivals" or "competitors," not enemies. Our language reserves "enemy" for more serious harm—physical or mental damage, economic distress, military defeat.

The desire to harm makes someone an enemy. That's why the word most properly applies to people, not abstractions. When we call "poverty" or "cancer" or "fascism" or "revolution" enemies, we are speaking metaphorically. In a war on poverty, or a crusade against cancer, we are trying to eliminate harmful conditions. These are not enemies to love, they are problems to solve. In this book we concentrate on people—people who may be fascists or revolutionaries, or they may be slum lords or torturers, or have any other reason for becoming our enemies.

"Enemy" implies staying power. An enemy's urge to hurt is not a passing fancy. It's a strong desire that persists, not a sudden outburst of anger. Even if the enemy changes and, for whatever reason, no longer has the desire to subdue me, the enmity between us tends to last because of my suspicions. If someone attacks me and later backs off and apologizes, I may well be slow to trust the change. Enmity is tenacious. It can outlast the lives of particular individuals and be passed on for generations. A French friend once told me, "It's easier for me today to get along with Germans than with the English. We French have only been fighting the Germans for the last hundred years, but we've been fighting the English for the last five hundred."

Enmity tends to be reciprocal. When I recognize that someone wants to hurt me, I react defensively. I want to remove the threat. During the 1984 convention of the National Organization for Women one delegate told a reporter, "We can't get bogged down arguing which Democratic candidate we're going to support. We've got to remember that Ronald Reagan is the enemy." She considered President Reagan harmful because of his administration's policies toward women. In labeling him the enemy she urged political action aimed at removing him from office. She wanted to defeat him.

When we look at these dynamics more closely, we see that enmity may start out existing only in the eye of the beholder. As I walk alone at night downtown, I spot a scowling young man across the street. I immediately think he might mug me. You never know these days. I'm on my guard, looking around for help, thinking how I might outmaneuver him. Now he's starting across the street toward me. Actually, he only wants to ask me for directions. He's not really my enemy, but I think he is. So I take preventive measures. I pull out my switchblade. Now his real intention may never become clear. "Hey, that guy is pointing a knife at me. I'd better take it away from him before somebody gets hurt." He attacks me. Hostility I only imagined before has become real.

Sooner or later we're all going to have some enemies. We may not like it. We try to avoid it. We would rather be skilled broken-field runners in human relations, sensing danger from this or that difficult person, taking clever evasive action. But no matter how artfully we navigate through the minefields of confrontation, we can't escape having enemies forever. Before figuring out ways to deal with our enemies, we need to look at how enemies happen. If we catch it early enough in the process, we can sometimes solve the problem with the proverbial ounce of prevention.

The three basic ways in which enmity begins are: 1) projection: one side without sufficient evidence imagines that the other side is hostile; 2) brutality: one party attacks without provocation; and 3) conflict: both sides want something and consider each other as obstacles. Often the three ways are present in differing degrees each time we find ourselves faced with an enemy. But it helps to understand each of them separately.

PROJECTION

One of the most common psychological mechanisms people have is to project an unpleasant characteristic on to others and then dislike them because of that characteristic. We often do this when we are unable to come to terms with some weakness in ourselves. If I am greedy, I can keep an eagle eye out for hints of avarice in others, and despise them for it. If I tend to be aggressive, I can magnify signs of menacing behavior in others, then denounce them for the cruelty I can't face in myself. If I'm ashamed of my sexuality, I can point to homosexuals or prostitutes, and feel clean when I consider them sinners.

We all have faults we don't like and that we have a hard time accepting. The psychologist Carl Jung called this part of us our "shadow." It's not easy to feel comfortable with all our warts and wrongdoings. Sometimes I don't even acknowledge these failings in myself. I repress them. I deny that I have them. But they pressure me, make me uneasy. I can alleviate the anxiety by perceiving these same flaws in others, and looking down on them for it. If I'm a poor workman, I blame my tools. Our crowd may want to control the neighborhood or dominate the world. But instead of coming to grips with ourselves we accuse others of wanting to control the neighborhood or dominate the world. Our side may have been guilty of wanton cruelty in the past, but instead of facing it and exorcizing it from our lives, we accuse the adversary of the very behavior we dislike in ourselves. In Jung's words, "It is in the nature of political bodies always to see the evil in the opposite group, just as the individual has an ineradicable tendency to get rid of everything he does not know and does not want to know about himself by foisting it off on somebody else."[1]

The Scapegoat   The late Thomas Merton described the projection process as a way of dealing with a sense of sin:

> We tend unconsciously to ease ourselves . . . of the
> burden of guilt that is in us, by passing it on to somebody
> else. . . . The temptation is, then, to account for my fault
> by seeing an equivalent amount of evil in someone else.
> Hence I minimize my own sins and compensate for do-
> ing so by exaggerating the faults of others.[2]

The original scapegoat ceremony described in the Bible involved the transferral of sins to an animal. "He [Aaron] is to lay both hands on the head of the live goat and confess over it all the wickedness and rebellion of the Israelites—all their sins—and put them on the goat's head. He shall send the goat away into the desert . . . . The goat will carry on itself all their sins" (Leviticus 16:21-22). The ritual's purpose was to lighten the load of guilt the people carried, and so relieve their fear of God's punishment.

It works. Scapegoating is not the best way to face life. But it's a pattern most people fall into fairly frequently, because it's a remarkably effective short-term remedy for anxiety. In the words of psychologist Robert Coles, "We crave scapegoats, targets to absorb our self-doubts, our feelings of worthlessness and hopelessness."[3] It works so well that it almost seems to be a natural process. According to psychoanalyst Israel Charny, "Knowing how to select a scapegoat and how to unload our feared weaknesses onto another seems rooted in our very being."[4]

During the later stages of the Vietnam War, American officials frequently engaged in scapegoating by alluding to the blood bath the enemy would cause if they gained control of that country. President Nixon said at a press conference, "If we withdraw from Vietnam and allow the enemy to come into Vietnam and massacre the civilians there by the millions, as they would—if we do that, let me say that America is finished insofar as the peacekeeper in the Asian world is concerned."[5] When he said that the enemy would massacre millions, he was reflecting the view of a majority of Americans who would rather think the worst of the other side than come to grips with slaughters perpetrated by U.S. forces, as at My Lai. And so we bombed those enemies heavily, and they fought back fiercely, "proving" that they were as bad as our leaders said they were.

Scapegoating is also the effect of another anxiety-reducing device known as displacement—transferring an emotion from its authentic object to a substitute. When a business executive, angry from an early-morning argument at home, lashes out at the office staff, the executive is shifting the anger from the spouse or children or whoever was involved in the domestic unpleasantness to another, more easily available target, the people at work. "What did we do to deserve this?" Nothing, of course. They have become scapegoats.

When things are going badly, it's fairly easy to find targets for blame. In the 1920s, many Germans, upset over their deteriorating economy and chafing over the huge reparations they had to pay after the First World War, accused communists—and later Jews—for causing their troubles.

Some scapegoats do in fact have the qualities being projected on them. At times people are greedy, or cruel, or lustful. The office staff does make mistakes. But this is not the decisive factor in the projection. It's a bonus that makes the scapegoater feel even better. "I came to the office on the prowl today, ready for a fight. When I found some of my people slacking off, wasting time, I really let them have it."

If we want to know that we are projecting rather than reacting, we have clues that can help. When we concentrate exclusively on the unpleasant traits in others without acknowledging failures in ourselves, we are projecting. The self-righteous "America First" proponent, constantly denouncing communist aggression, is projecting. When we use the undesirable action of others as an excuse for similar actions ourselves, we are projecting. The guardian of public morals who searches out and examines obscene material to protect others from it is projecting. This doesn't mean that others' offensive behavior is purely imaginary, but it does mean the projector's response is dictated more by inner emotional imbalance than by the perceived irregularities.

The Stranger   Unfamiliar people are natural targets for projection and displacement. Hostility toward strangers is an ancient phenomenon. It's sometimes called fear of the unknown. We easily imagine unpleasant characteristics in people we don't know anything about. When strangers speak a foreign language, wear odd clothes, have a strikingly different appearance, our first reaction is to think of them as inferior. "They don't do things the way we do, so they're not as good as we are." And if they're not as good as we are, they might be dangerous.

Into the tiny Alpine village strides a tall, bearded man, clad in sheepskin, armed with a walking staff, a knife in his belt. He stops in the town square and looks around. The villagers peer out their windows cautiously. Nobody knows him. Some think he's a menace. "Hide the women and children." Some think he's a robber. "Bar the doors."

They have nothing to go on; they've never seen him before. The truth of the matter is that he's a decent family man who has been lost in the mountains for months after straying from his hunting party. All he wants to do is find his way back home. He's looking for help. But the villagers don't know this. They don't ask him why he's there. Nothing interferes with their suspicions. Small signs of danger on the stranger's part—a dark look, a sudden move, a hand to his knife—give grounds for their fear.

The stranger's suspected hostility may well turn out to be real. Perceiving the cautious quiet, the negative atmosphere of the village, he feels threatened. "Obviously the folks here are pretty nasty. I'd better get out fast." He starts to run, brushing aside a child who has wandered into the street. "Look, he hit that little girl. He really is dangerous. Come on, everybody, let's get him." They treat him like an enemy, and he becomes one. He fights back, hurting some of them with his staff before escaping into the hills.

Many a shipload of European explorers landed on shores in the Americas to find bronze-skinned natives standing silently, staring inscrutably. They projected on these strange looking inhabitants the exploitative aggressiveness they had themselves. At the slightest sign of hostility they began to

attack with swords and muskets, a preventive strike. In retaliation, and in their own self-protective desire to push the foreigners back into the sea, many native peoples became real
enemies. The European scapegoaters felt vindicated. "These
savages are just as bad as we suspected."

It's easy for me to be hostile to a particular stranger
when others around me are thinking the same way. Everybody
on the ship knows that European Christians are superior to
New World heathens. All my neighbors are talking about
Jewish bankers bleeding our fatherland. The people I talk to
all agree that the communists will cause a blood bath in
Vietnam.

When reality-testing contact with strangers is limited
or nonexistent, our projections can go unchallenged. For years
after the creation of the state of Israel, the image of Israelis
shared by most Egyptians was of predatory, land-grabbing
foreigners. There had been no diplomatic relations, no travel
between the countries, no person-to-person contact except on
the battlefield. Shortly after tensions were relaxed following
the 1979 Camp David accords, a planeload of Israeli reporters
landed in Cairo. The Egyptians were pleasantly surprised to
see that the press representatives were decent, enthusiastic
people. Their image of Israelis, reinforced by decades of isolation, gave way to an accurate assessment of the human qualities of their former enemies.

Enemy Thinking   When I'm overly suspicious of people,
doubt their integrity, believe without evidence that they're out
to get me, I'm indulging in enemy thinking. Enemy thinking
happens when I'm quick to fasten upon slights, when I inter-
pret a careless remark as a personal affront. I'm doing enemy
thinking when I attribute disreputable motives to people of
whose actions I disapprove. A neighbor builds a fence. "They
want to keep us out." That's enemy thinking, if what they really
want to do is keep their dogs in.

Enemy thinking also occurs when I'm so totally sure
of the rightness of my position that I know that those who
oppose it are wrong. I don't have to wonder about their
motives, because I see what they're doing. If I come home in

the middle of the day and find an old pickup truck in my driveway half full of my furniture, my immediate thought is that those two men I see inside my house are robbing me.

They may be, but first I'd better make sure that I'm not conjuring up something on my own. Maybe those two men really are stealing my furniture. But before I go in with guns blazing, I would be better advised to enlist the help of the local police to check out the remote possibility that they are hired movers who have entered the wrong house by mistake.

Enemy thinking is an important factor in enemy making. It can lead to ill-advised steps, setting off the now familiar dynamics of provocation and defensive aggression. The carloads of teenagers who congregate at night in the church parking lot across the street may be planning to terrorize the neighborhood. Or I may be engaging in enemy thinking. If I get several large friends with shotguns and growling dogs to clear them out, I may be creating the very enemies I had hoped to eliminate.

Stereotyping is another form of enemy thinking. We do this when we attribute to all people in a particular category the unpleasant characteristics that may exist in a few. "Poor people are lazy." "The rich are greedy." "Blacks are violent." "Whites are racists." Stereotyping follows the same pattern as hostility to strangers. It's socially reinforced. It can also easily go unchallenged because we tend not to associate with people we've adversely characterized.

When I recognize that I am engaging in enemy thinking, I can handle the situation better, I can defuse it before the other side picks up on what's happening. And I'm better prepared to handle the enemy thinking others might be doing about me. I should be able to cope with their hostile behavior more realistically and not automatically resort to defensive countermeasures. But if neither of us realizes that enemy thinking is going on, the hostility invariably escalates.

BRUTALITY

The second major source of enemies is others' aggressive behavior toward us that we've done nothing to provoke. They become enemies on their own. In recent decades considerable study has been devoted to the phenomenon of individual and collective aggression. The Nazi terror was the most appalling instance in human history. But we daily read of savage beatings, rape, cold-blooded murder, and misplaced military heroics that leave homes burning and families dying. We know more about what's happening when someone wants to hurt me, gain power over me, see me suffer—and so, by definition, becomes my enemy.

Sadism   Some brutality is an expression of that personality disorder called sadism. People afflicted with this condition look around for somebody to beat up, physically or emotionally. They are able to gain a sense of adequacy within themselves only when they feel others are inferior. One way to make them inferior is to punch them into submission, or bully them into cowing.

Sadism is usually the result of prior humiliation, internalized as resentment. Most sadists were abused as children, or repressed by overly zealous discipline at school, in military service, or in prison. Their resentment is not directed against those who caused their misery. Rather they make someone else closer at hand, someone who appears weaker, their victim. The sadistic person is saying, in effect, "I don't feel very good, but I'll be better if I know you feel worse than I do. So I'm going to put you in that condition."

Hurting another is satisfying because it overcomes the feeling of being impotent and vulnerable. Many rapes result from this kind of frustration. A twenty-three-year-old man who admitted he would like to assault women described his urge: "Just the fact that they can come up to me and just melt me and make me feel like a dummy makes me want revenge . . . I feel that they have power over me just by their presence . . . . They have power over me so I want power over them."[6] The typical rapist is a man whose personal power is in question. Doubts about his own strength make him want to do violence to women. His goal is power, not sex. Women seem to him an easy mark because they're physically vulnerable. So, by an act of sexual violence, he proves to himself that he really is strong.

Once violence begins the aggressor may slip into a rage. It's not rationally directed toward the victim, but it's a feeling of heightened joy, like being drunk with power. Psychoanalyst Erich Fromm described it as an outburst of fury that attempts to overcome the existential burden of powerlessness and separateness "by achieving a trancelike state of ecstasy ('to be beside oneself') and thus to regain unity within oneself."[7] The urge to experience this ecstasy may be at work in bullies, rapists, or torturers.

Fear   It's difficult to penetrate behind the facade of someone who is being brutal. Our initial tendency is to label the enemy's viciousness as pure evil. But if we find out what's really going on with a sadist, we may well discover a weak ego struggling to overcome feelings of inadequacy. Or we may find sheer fear. I may not have done anything threatening, but something about my personality, perhaps, causes others to feel diminished. Or maybe their fear is totally without external foundation. They are so lost and lonely that they are incapable of dealing adequately with the pressures of life. They suffer from the emotional disorder known as paranoia.

In the summer of 1983 a man on trial for killing three students at Cleveland State University tried to explain his actions to the judge. Although the three victims were total strangers, he said he killed them because he was waging a guerrilla war against blacks and Jews, whom he considered his enemies.[8] Such a paranoid person suffers from an intense feeling of fear, but can't readily locate its cause. The logical portion of the personality says that the fear must be due to an external threat. The paranoid person looks around for someone who appears to be dangerous, and always "finds" the threat.

Fear, whether the danger is real or only imagined, leads initially to flight—get away from the trouble. But if flight is not possible, or not chosen for any number of reasons—pride, perhaps, or a desire to remove the threat for good—fear can lead to active hostility. Becoming aggressive is one of the most effective ways of dealing with fear. When a fearful person begins to attack, the painful nature of fright can momentarily disappear, overcome by the energy of action.

The paranoid person looks on the aggressive action as self-defense. The jarring impact on the aggressor's psyche from inflicting harm is softened by the conviction that the harm is necessary to escape the threat. Fear is a potent source of aggressive behavior. It turns many people into enemies. When aggression toward me incites me to a self-defensive action in response, I then "prove" to the aggressor that I pose a real threat. The unfortunate projection-protection cycle begins.

CONFLICT

It's helpful to understand the pure instances in which enmity is provoked by us or caused solely by the other side. But most enmity does not arise unilaterally. It develops from a conflict we find ourselves in, which one or both of us wants to win badly enough that we're willing to hurt the other.

Conflicts occur when vectors of human activity intersect so that one interferes with the other. When two children reach for the same piece of pie, they're in what sociologists call a conflict over resource scarcity—in which the supply of pie is limited so both children can't have all they want. Other conflicts involve position scarcity. When two adults reach for the same promotion at work, or two teams battle for the same championship, they're after one status that can't at the same time serve them both.

If the conflict takes place within agreed limits, we call it competition, and think of it as healthy. Competition sharpens our skills, intensifies our interest, and increases our potential for growth. But when competition breaks out of the limits, when an attitude of "all's fair in love and war" takes over, competition becomes conflict, and enemies can be made. The two children who want the pie or the two adults who want the job need not become enemies, but they can. And they will, if either side starts up the projection-protection cycle.

When I wake up in the middle of the night to hear prowlers in my home, I'm in a conflict. If I close my eyes and pretend to be asleep, they may leave without hurting me. But I want to defend my family. So I reach into my nightstand drawer and pull out a gun. Now my defensive action threatens them. They see me as their enemy, because I want to hurt them. If they don't leave, I'm prepared to shoot. The intruders may indeed turn around and run out. But they're more likely to try to get the gun away from me, or use their own weapons to neutralize me. Their initial enmity, breaking in to rob me, has taken on some self-justification. They want to save their lives. However a conflict starts, both parties can focus on the self-defense dimension to increase the hostility.

Life is peppered with conflicts. But conflict itself is not the problem. We can escape conflict only if we escape all human interaction. And if we could, a conflict-free life would be dull, even deadly. The challenge is not to escape conflict, but to wage it constructively, in a way that does not produce enemies. Later we'll examine some positive techniques for doing this. Right now we're trying to understand the hazards in the path. Some of them stem directly from the complications of group dynamics.

Tribalism   Others may have nothing against me personally, but they're opposed to a group to which I belong. They may hate me because I'm a capitalist. They think of capitalists as greedy exploiters of the world's resources. Or they may dislike me because I'm a man, and they view men as callous, domineering brutes. Others may despise me because I'm white. They remember how whites enslaved their ancestors and now see whites running a society that locks them into second-class citizenship. Some resent me as a North American, who luxuriates in comforts gained largely at their expense. All who feel this way about me are hostile to me because I'm in a particular category. If they know me at all they may think I'm a pretty decent person. But my group threatens them, so they oppose me. They see a conflict, even if I may not.

I can understand how they feel when I put the shoe on my foot. I don't like the idea of somebody menacing my people, either. And I'm part of many associations. Some are based on family ties, ethnic backgrounds, or residential patterns.

Others I seek out more directly, like church membership, professional exchanges, or solidarity in a common cause. Our tendency to gather in helpful clusters makes us want to protect these interests against outside forces. In doing so I'm not just defending myself, which can seem egotistical, but I'm concerned about my family, my friends, my society, or, more noble still, our ideals, our principles. My desire to defend is directed more toward the good of others than toward myself. It seems beautiful, even selfless. The altruism intensifies my dedication to the group, increases my readiness to defend it. *The New Yorker* magazine noted that "The most enduring causes of the organized violence we call war is not ideology or greed, but the potent mixture of fear and allegiance which breeds intense tribal rivalries."[9]

The mixture of fear and allegiance becomes even more potent if we fall into what sociologists call ethnocentrism— thinking of our group as superior to others. Fromm called it "group narcissism."[10] It happens when we look on our family or church or team or gang or nation as the greatest, to compensate for our own weakness and insecurity. "We're Number One." I alone may not be, but my group is. And I feel fine as part of it. So I'm extra sensitive to threats against it. Whatever their source, we had better be on our guard, prepared to defend ourselves. My people need to be protected against "them"—even if we don't know clearly who "they" are. The English writer Daniel Defoe once said that there were a hundred thousand stout countryfellows in his time ready to fight to the death against popery, "without knowing whether popery was a man or a horse."

Nationalism   Group narcissism can be especially potent when it takes the form of nationalism. This distortion of patriotism elevates one's country above all other values. Love of country is high on everyone's list of virtues. Extolled in Sir Walter Scott's immortal lines, "Breathes there a man with soul so dead who never to himself has said, this is my own, my native land," patriotism seeks the genuine good of one's country. But when we're personally more uncertain than confident, more fearful of our failures than secure in our accomplishments, we tend to push hard to assert ourselves. We neglect to place our country in the context of the community of nations, refuse to acknowledge that our welfare includes respect for the rights of other peoples.

Group narcissism expressed as national self-admiration waxes strong in the face of an enemy. Senator William Fulbright saw it during the Vietnam era. Our national preoccupation with being the "biggest" and the "greatest" nation, he wrote, suggests "an underlying lack of confidence in ourselves, a supposition that unless we are 'No. 1' we will be nothing: worthless and despised."[11] More recently, former Ambassador to the Soviet Union George Kennan expressed the same conviction. "It seems to me the air of this country is filled with a great deal of rhetoric . . . of self-admiration and self-righteousness. We seem to have to feel we need to reassure ourselves constantly of how fine we are, how virtuous we are, how wonderful we are. And for that we need some other country that is exactly the opposite."[12]

So we locate an enemy. And we're ready to fight, to prove ourselves. It doesn't matter much how the conflict started. We have an enemy, so we'll show ourselves how good we are by standing up against it. Put those missiles in Europe. Defeat communism in Central America. We wish the enemy had sent teams to the Olympics so we could have trounced them there, too. We identify with Stephen Decatur's toast after the naval action against the Barbary pirates in 1818: "Our country. In her intercourse with foreign nations, may she always be right. But our country, right or wrong." Group narcissism elevates one's country above other moral concerns. "I'll not only die for my country, but I'll kill for it." Death squads in El Salvador routinely assassinated people they accused of being "enemies of the fatherland."

Having an identifiable enemy produces some clear benefits for any society. It draws the members closer together, serves as a basis of unity among them. It gives them a convenient scapegoat to blame when things go wrong. As long as the enemy is kept at a distance and never actually attacks, its existence is invigorating.

But it's also dangerous, because it fails to come to grips

with the emotional imbalance underlying the need for an enemy. It's dangerous especially to those outsiders who fill the role of enemy, because it places them in jeopardy. But it's dangerous even to the members of the society themselves, who become victims as the enemy defends itself through counter-attacks.

Power Drive   Inter-group conflict brings into play the complicated energies of many individuals. Leaders often have, in Washington analyst Richard Barnet's term, "well-developed power drives."[13] When they feel their control is weak they try to consolidate their position, increase their command. One effective ploy is to proclaim the existence of an enemy out there. "Forget our differences. We have to close ranks and pull together to defend ourselves. Stay the course. Follow me." Internal problems recede, supplanted by the urgency of protecting ourselves from dangers outside. In this light we can understand the advice Secretary of State William Henry Seward gave to President Abraham Lincoln shortly before the outbreak of the Civil War. He suggested dealing with the rising unrest at home by adopting a vigorous foreign policy which included the possibility of declaring war on Spain or France.[14] We saw the same device at work when the Ayatollah Khomeini took power in Iran. He encouraged his fellow Iranians to look on the United States as the "Great Satan," responsible for whatever ailed their society.

In 1982 the world witnessed a small-scale war over the Falkland Islands. Argentina's military government, whose repressive measures were causing increasing internal unrest, tried to rally its people against the European colonial power which controlled those islands, their Malvinas. By stirring up war fever the generals hoped to counteract the internal dissatisfaction over the thousands of those who had "disappeared"—people kidnapped and murdered by government agents. The enemy they chose to confront was ironically having troubles of its own. Britain's Prime Minister Margaret Thatcher had aroused considerable controversy with her economic policies. Most Britons momentarily forgot their domestic problems in the aura of martial self-righteousness that swept the country.

It worked—for England. Its surprisingly decisive victory increased the Thatcher government's popularity at home. The Argentine generals, on the other hand, lost their gamble. Within a year some were court-martialed; the rest were ousted from office and replaced by a civilian government.

A power drive is often directed toward money as a means of dominance. Not political power but accumulated wealth is sought to assure a sense of superiority. A nation's missile makers need a serious threat. To insure a continuing demand for their products a perpetual crisis atmosphere must be fostered. The enemy is omnipresent. It is portrayed as strong, and getting stronger.

Neurotic Obedience   The other side of the coin of the power drive is the assent of those who follow. Obedience to established authority is necessary for the smooth functioning of any society. Social education stresses its importance. "Obey the law." "Respect authority." Obedience is equated with virtue, disobedience with sin. Many live within this framework because they know it's for the common good. Others are driven by what psychologists call authoritarian personalities. They are happy to take orders. It relieves them of the anxiety of making their own decisions and accepting the consequences of their own initiatives. They want to submit to someone else, and will often do so regardless of whether the authority figure is right or wrong. Their emotional needs override their common sense and lead them docilely to accept the leaders' dictates. When those in authority are operating not so much for the common weal as for their own self-aggrandizement or megalomania, authoritarian personalities will still obey. The combination often leads to aggressive action against those designated by the leaders as enemies.

A motorcycle gang threatens a family. A member of a liberation movement plants a bomb in a department store. An army mobilizes on the borders, poised for an attack. A heightened group consciousness, idealized as devotion to the cause, usually drives people who take part in such acts of aggression. Many receive a personal boost when they are part of the action. Fromm called it "conformist aggression." He said that the need to conform serves to "mobilize aggressive impulses that otherwise might not have become manifest . . . The impulse . . . not to conform constitutes for many a real threat, against which they defend themselves by performing the required aggressive act."[15]

The violence is rationalized. The harassing motorcycle gang believes it is displaying its power, heightening its prestige. The terrorists plant their bombs as an act of war for the freedom of their people. The recruits flock to the front confident that they are fighting for God's cause, or to preserve their homes from fanatical invaders. These acts of violence can provide significant psychic income. Charny notes that "a nation joined in the common task of defense is a nation enriched with a sense of purpose that puts a spring in many a man's step . . . More than a few individuals actually relish war as it puts an end to their unbearable, unspoken inner terrors of nothingness and meaninglessness."[16]

Dehumanization   Normally a whole cluster of feelings— fear, compassion, guilt, shame—arise when we cause other human beings, even enemies, to suffer. We have to escape these feelings if we are to mount an effective attack—or counter- attack. One common way of reducing anxiety is to view enemies as different. When we think of them as not quite belonging to the human family, as lacking some essential characteristics, we consider that they are not really as deserv- ing of life as we are. Then if it's necessary to attack them, we can handle it without guilt.

Dehumanization of enemies is common. The British could more easily subdue the native peoples of Asia and Africa when they saw them as subhuman. The poet Kipling so de- scribed them when he urged shouldering the White Man's Burden: bring civilization to "your new-caught, sullen peo- ple, half-devil and half-child." Nineteenth century rhetoric characterized native Americans as savages and brutes. During the First World War a congressional representative painted a derogatory picture of Germans: "The cave man has once again broken loose upon the world. He is mad and crazy. He knows not the impulses of humanity;. . . he feels not the sentiments of truth or sympathy or justice; he is bent on the unwavering course of brute force, pillage, and murder. That cave man is the crazy German Emperor, and the heartless Prussian military caste."[17]

American propaganda after Pearl Harbor portrayed the Japanese as little slant-eyed monsters. *Time* magazine entitled its story of the battle of Iwo Jima "Rodent Extermination." An ad in the *New York Times* pictured a toothy Japanese face with the headline "Rat Poison Wanted." A few years later an editorial in another New York newspaper called Nikita Khrushchev, symbol of our enemy in the Cold War, "a pig in human form." Chinese were the Yellow Peril, like a disease. Vietnamese became "gooks." American patrols in Vietnam often went "skunk hunting," or engaged in a "turkey shoot." During the electronic phase late in that war the enemy showed up as blips on a radar screen. And, as one observer put it, "a blip is worse than a gook."[18]

Another form of dehumanization presents the enemy as superhuman: crafty, cunning, and cruel. Tens of thousands of women persecuted as witches were accused of being under the influence of the devil.[19] This liaison supposedly gave them extraordinary powers to harm—induce disease, use the evil eye, cause injury. Nazi propaganda often depicted Jews with a similar superhuman liaison: they were agents of Satan, diabolically bent on weakening the Reich.

Our Cold War adversaries often seemed to have superhuman powers, or so we imagined from such descriptions as this in the 1950s: "The ruthless Stalin . . . is preparing his armies for world domination . . . Not satisfied with conquest of his own countrymen, this monster has set forth a master plan for world conquest. Stalin is fighting to destroy all religion, our allies, and our way of life.[20] Mao Zedong and Ho Chi Minh appeared on a political poster in the mid-1960s like characters from a Japanese monster movie: ravenous, fanged, with burning eyes, outstretched arms and clawed fingers, leaning over a map of Southeast Asia. One still hears, in Soviet rhetoric, references to the United States as fiendishly clever, militarily superior, intent on conquering the world if the restraining forces were relaxed even slightly.

Desensitization   A much used desensitizing mechanism is to refuse to think about—or even deny—the human suffering we are causing the enemy. B-52 bombadiers concentrated on their electronic display screens, not the civilians who were dying as a result of their actions. Missile crews may choose to believe that they are aiming at purely military objects. Or, more likely, they suppress thoughts about the targets at all and concentrate on the technical skills they must employ to launch their "birds."

Another way to block one's sense of responsibility is to pass it off to superiors in the chain of command. "The higher-ups know what they're doing. It must be all right or they wouldn't have set things up like this. All we're doing is following orders." Military people are encouraged to think of themselves not as killers, but as cogs in a machine, parts of a system, members of a team. The engineers who design the death machines never use them. The middle managers who organize the logistics do not make the overall policies. As Richard Barnet put it, "Those who plan do not kill, and those who kill do not plan." He called the overall system the "bureaucratization of homicide."[21]

The Nazis developed what they called "Language Rules" in communicating about their genocide against the Jews.[22] Their official word for the mass murder was "final solution." Instead of "killing," they were to say "special treatment." They deliberately distorted words in this way to help keep an emotional distance from what they were doing. We see the same need to resort to euphemisms in other enemy contexts. CIA jargon for murdering a no longer useful agent is "terminating with extreme prejudice." Going to war becomes "use of the military instrument." A bombing run is "a surgical strike." The hydrogen bomb on the tip of a missile is "the physics package." The nose cone which contains it is "the hardware." Citizens of an enemy country become its "political assets." Killing them is a "counter-value strike." Language like this helps suppress images of flaming enemy children, torn enemy bodies, shattered enemy skulls.

The net result of the enemy atmosphere is a powerful social climate where what is wrong in normal times becomes right, what was illegal becomes legal, and where otherwise ordinary people, even the best and the brightest, can support mass killing. The processes of making and maintaining enemies are supported by forces deep within our human psyche and social fabric. Until we understand them we're going to be under their influence. But understanding is an important step toward changing them.

DISCUSSION QUESTIONS

These questions are designed to stimulate critical thinking and expand the reader's understanding of the ideas presented in each chapter. They may also serve as a basis for group discussions.

1. List several persons or groups of persons whom you know to be enemies in your life right now—enemies in the sense of wanting to "do ill" to you.

2. What nations do our political leaders consider to be enemies of the United States at this time?

3. Can you see in any of these enemies elements of the scapegoat syndrome, or of hostility to strangers?

4. When was the last time you came across an instance of "enemy thinking"—in casual conversations, Letters to the Editor, etc.?

5. One occasionally hears the slogan, "Question authority." In what sense is this a helpful piece of advice? How far should it be carried?

CHAPTER TWO

TWO MYTHS,
TWO MENTALITIES

In our unfolding, life-long education, much of what we store in our mental reservoir as fact or truth is in reality the legacy of those who have influenced us along the way. Sociologist Peter Berger pointed out that "Most of what we 'know' we have taken on the authority of others, and it is only as others continue to confirm this 'knowledge' that it continues to be plausible to us." He was referring to "facts" that are beyond most people's ability to verify empirically, like "The earth revolves around the sun." He was also referring to "truths" that represent value judgments of a particular society, like "Communism (or Capitalism) is a harmful economic system." Berger rightly noted that "it is such socially shared, socially taken-for-granted 'knowledge' that allows us to move with a measure of confidence through everyday life."[1]

Some of that "knowledge" consists of religious beliefs and world-explaining stories, which speak directly to our deeper, more complex needs. These beliefs and stories are "myths" in the proper sense of the word. To call them myths does not imply that they are false. It rather means that they are powerful views of reality that engage us in the depths of our minds and hearts. Whether they are true or false is not in question. Myths in this sense provide a graspable representation of the mysteries surrounding human existence. They support and inspire us.

All of us learn myths in this sense as we grow up. For many of us the Biblical story of creation is one. "In the beginning God created the heavens and the earth. Now the earth was formless and empty, darkness was over the surface of the deep, and the Spirit of God was hovering over the waters. And God said, 'Let there be light,' and there was light" (Genesis 1:1-3). This reverent recital conveys an image of the world and everything in it coming into being by the creative act of a transcendent, superior power. Scientifically, we don't know how the universe got started. It's a genuine mystery. Cosmologists give us theories of big bangs and oscillating eons, but nobody has the proven answer yet. The Biblical account gives us a satisfying image of the mystery which lets us rest with it.

Myths also serve the important function of legitimating everyday activities by placing them in the context of universal patterns. We see ourselves repeating a sequence that is "natural," and gain reassurance that we are living correctly. God created the world in six days and rested on the seventh. It's only right for us, then, to look forward to weekends off.

People act differently when influenced by different myths. In the religion-dominated city of Jerusalem Jewish business stops on Saturday, the Biblical Sabbath. Christian stores are closed on Sunday, the day of Jesus' resurrection. Moslem shops are shut on Friday, the day of congregational prayer designated by Mohammed.

The Hindu religion contains a creation story different from the Biblical one. "In the beginning this was being alone,

one only, without a second. It thought, May I be many, may I grow forth. It sent forth fire. That fire thought, May I be many, may I grow forth. It sent forth water . . . That water thought, May I be many, may I grow forth. It sent forth food . . ."[2] In this myth the world comes into existence by action from within. In the beginning everything was undifferentiated Being. Being's thought was the creating power. It brought about the array of elements we see in the universe around us.

We have no way of proving scientifically that either of these creation myths is true. Both give a vivid picture of the origins of the universe. Both give an image which allows some peace with the mystery. But they have significantly different implications for all of us. One leads to worship of a transcendent Creator. The other calls for awed reverence for nature. One points directly to a personal God who reveals designs for living. The other implies a pantheistic appreciation of the world and a searching for supernatural secrets within it.

The Judaeo-Christian story, enshrined in the Bible, is taught to those who grow up under the influence of synagogue or church. The Hindu story, enshrined in the Vedas, is taught to those who grow up in India and elsewhere under the influence of that sacred book. It's possible for someone who starts out believing one myth to change and accept the other. But such a change is difficult. It begins with understanding that the myth which has dominated one's life until now is not the only adequate interpretation of reality, that there are others, and that one of them might be even more appropriate.

Since enemies have always been a fact of life, we would expect that myths have developed to help us deal with them. In fact, two distinct collections, mythologies, have been around for a long time. We can call them the War Myth and the Peace Myth.

We know that conflicts occur. Enemies arise. In the War Myth the best way to meet them is to be tough, put them down—by force, if necessary. In the Peace Myth the best way to meet enemies is to be patient, sidestep their violence, and direct one's efforts to healing human hurts wherever we find them. Which of these patterns predominates in an individual sets the tone for that person dealing with whatever enemies are encountered along the way. Like creation myths, it's possible to start out under the influence of one, then later change and consciously accept the guidance of the other.

THE WAR MYTH

The foundation for War Myths is a view of our human environment as a jungle. A human being is "a beast of prey," wrote the German philosopher Oswald Spengler. He believed that others will try to dominate us unless we are strong and prepared to fight back. This belief has a long history. The ancient historian Thucydides thought that people are disposed to take advantage of others: "Of the gods we believe and of men we know that, by a law of their nature, whatever they can rule they will." This means, he wrote, that "the powerful exact what they can and the weak grant what they must." He saw this as an ineradicable reality of our existence: "This law was not made by us, and we are not the first to have acted upon it; we did but inherit it."[3] Unless people are restrained, goes this view, they will try to control and dominate others. Life is a constant struggle. Those who are not with us are against us. The only alternatives are to overcome or be overcome. We've got to be ready to fight. "If you want peace, prepare for war," as the old Roman adage had it.

   The early books of the Bible portray God leading the Hebrew people out of slavery into a promised land. When they get there they find other people already established in the area. The Israelites want to take possession of the land. They see these ensconced inhabitants as obstacles to the fulfillment of God's promise. A conflict ensues—two peoples vying for the same territory. They become enemies of each other. God proposes a definite way for the Israelites to deal with these enemies. Make slaves of them if you can, or kill them if they resist. "When you march up to attack a city, make its people an offer of peace. If they accept and open their gates, all the people in it shall be subject to forced labor and shall work for you. If they refuse to make peace and engage you in battle, lay siege to that city. When the Lord your God delivers it into your hand, put to the sword all the men in it. As for the women, the children, the livestock and everything else in the city, you may take these as plunder for yourselves" (Deuteronomy 20:10-14).

Although Biblical scholars often stress that such commands applied only to those wars fought under the express command of God for the very existence of the Chosen People,[4] they did provide a pattern for ancient Israel's wars against its neighbors. The Bible describes the Israelites carrying out this kind of destruction repeatedly against the Canaanites, Amalekites, Jebusites, and other native peoples in their conquest of the promised land. After taking the city of Jericho, for example, they "destroyed with the sword every living thing in it—men and women, young and old, cattle and sheep and donkeys" (Joseph 6:21). Some of their prophets promised that following the pattern would eventually lead to a world kingdom where all nations will either acknowledge the supremacy of Israel or be killed: "Foreigners will rebuild your walls, and their kings will serve you . . . Your gates will always stand open . . . so that men may bring you the wealth of nations—their kings led in triumphal procession. For the kingdom that will not serve you will perish; it will be utterly ruined" (Isaiah 60:10-12). The basic idea in the War Myth is that opposition must be overcome, and the most effective way to overcome it is by force.

The New Testament has a version of the War Myth. It is found in the last book, Revelation. In scarcely veiled symbolism the visionary John portrays Rome as a beast in the service of Satan (Revelation 13:1-4), and boldly proclaims the destruction of that evil empire. In a climactic scene Rome and its allies, "the kings of the whole world," are gathered together by demons "for the battle on the great day of God almighty" in "the place that in Hebrew is called Armageddon (Revelation 15:14,16). Arrayed against them are the forces of heaven. "I saw heaven standing open and there before me was a white horse whose rider is called Faithful and True . . . The armies of heaven were following him, riding on white horses and dressed in fine linen, white and clean" (Revelation 19:11,14).

Although the book of Revelation does not describe the battle itself, the outcome was clear. The good side won, and won decisively. The kings of the earth and their armies "were killed with the sword that came out of the mouth of the rider on the horse, and all the birds gorged themselves on their flesh" (Revelation 19:21). The beast, Rome, is thrown alive into the fiery lake of burning sulfur. There, along with Satan, its master, it "will be tormented day and night for ever and ever" (Revelation 20:10).

This vision of vengeance undoubtedly proved emotionally satisfying to many Christians. Although the myth of Armageddon does not counsel aggressive human action against enemies, it does suggest that evil people will eventually be overcome in a cosmic conflict by means of heroic, heavenly violence. This mythical image persisted in Christian consciousness. It emerged from time to time to reinforce an attitude of self-righteousness in the face of hostile forces which could be identified as enemies of God.

The mythology of pre-Christian Europe on the whole featured earthly as well as heavenly force. Wodin, after whom the fourth day of our week is named, was an important Teutonic god. He was pictured armed with a shining breastplate and a golden helmet, holding a spear which had been forged by dwarfs and was unerringly accurate. One of his important roles was to do battle against foes. And he always won. Wodin-inspired warriors fought vigorously against opposing tribes. If they died in battle they believed they would end up in Valhalla, the heavenly banquet hall where the god rewarded fallen heroes.

In the new Europe that grew out of the ruins of the Roman Empire, tribal peoples accepted Christian baptism. But they also retained their lusty readiness to take up arms to solve problems. They interpreted Christian symbols to conform with their deep-rooted convictions. Clovis, the first of these chieftains to be converted to Christianity, saw Jesus as a war god who gave him victory in battle. He once said that if he and his men had been around at the time of Pontius Pilate, Jesus would never have been crucified.[5]

Saint Peter was a favorite of the Franks, because he had

used his weapon in his master's defense. The Normans liked Saint Michael the Archangel with his flaming sword. He had walloped the fallen angels in a big battle in heaven. They gave his name to their island fortress, Mont St. Michel. Saint George the dragon-slayer, who if he didn't exist had to be invented, became the patron of England. Spain took as its model Saint James, a Son of Thunder, who had once asked that fire be called down from heaven to incinerate a particularly recalcitrant village (Luke 9:54).

CRUSADES

The War Myth tends to eliminate gray areas. You're either right or wrong, on God's side or the other side. Some of its variations owe much to the ancient Persian religion we know as Zoroastrianism. This belief pictured a supreme god, Ahura Mazda ("Wise Lord"), ruling over the kingdom of light. At the same time a powerful sinister being, Angra Mainyu ("Evil Spirit"), controls a supernatural kingdom of darkness. The world of human beings is a battleground between the forces of good and light on the one hand and the forces of evil and darkness on the other, each seeking to gain the supreme domination. Humans can engage in the struggle on either side. After they die the Wise Lord will judge them on whether they have sided with right or wrong, light or darkness. Those who have chosen wisely, who are on the right side, can be confident that their opponents are agents of the Evil Spirit. If we're on the side of good, those opposing us must be on the side of evil. It helps in fighting against them to be convinced that they deserve the damage they're about to get from us. They do indeed if they're evil. And we know they're evil since they're not on the same side as we are.

This Persian myth influenced a North African religious sect known as the Manicheans, whose best known member, before his conversion to Christianity, was Augustine of Hippo. Through Saint Augustine's influential writings traces of the Manichean myth found their way into mainstream Christian thinking. It showed up in the tendency to divide reality between good and evil, and to see the other side, whoever they might happen to be at the time, as evil. Given an appropriate enemy, the Manichean myth coupled with the European warrior tradition led to a crusading mentality against those who could be labeled enemies of God.

In Europe these were easily identifiable: Jews, first and foremost, then heretics of every stripe, and later, after the Reformation, Catholics as agents of the Anti-Christ Pope, or Protestants as deformers of the True Church. But medieval Christians found their major enemy outside Europe in those Middle Eastern people who had embraced the religion of the prophet Mohammed. Oblivious to the central tenet of Islam that peace comes through submission to God, the Powerful One, Allah, European crusaders called them infidels, unbelievers, and set out on a determined campaign to crush them.

Some church leaders saw the Moslem menace not only as a threat to Christendom, but also as a splendid opportunity for channeling against outsiders those war energies that were debilitating Europe. Pope Urban II expressed both ideas when he called the first Crusade during the Council of Clermont in 1095: "O race of the Franks, we learn that in some of your provinces no one can venture on the road by day or by night without injury or attack by highwaymen, and no one is secure even at home. Let us then re-enact the law of our ancestors known as the Truce of God. And now that you have promised to maintain the peace among yourselves, you are obligated to succor your brethren in the East, menaced by an accursed race, utterly alienated from God. The Holy Sepulchre of our Lord is polluted by the filthiness of an unclean nation . . . Let all hatred depart from among you, all quarrels end, all wars cease. Start upon the road to the Holy Sepulchre to wrest that land from the wicked race and subject it to yourselves."[6]

The crowd enthusiastically responded, *Deus vult*, "God wills it." The crusaders set out, marching under the sign of the cross. The word crusade comes from the Latin *cruciata*, marked with a cross—because of the blue and red emblem sewn on the front of the solders' tunics. They marched to a holy war, as confident as their ancient Hebrew forebears that God was on their side. They now had an enemy upon whom they could let loose the fury of their feelings—infidels, God's enemies. Churchmen urged people to join the cause. "In the death of a pagan a Christian is exultant, because Christ is glorified," preached Bernard of Clairvaux to the Knights Templar."[7]

One elated commander described the slaughter crusaders inflicted on the people of Jerusalem. "Some of our men . . . cut off the heads of their enemies; others tortured them longer by casting them into the flames. Piles of heads, hands, and feet were to be seen in the streets of the city . . . This day, I say, marks the justification of all Christianity and the humiliation of paganism."[8] As John Calvin was later to write, no consideration should be paid to humanity when the honor of God was at stake.

Medieval theologians like Thomas Aquinas defended the killing. "Christ's faithful often wage war with unbelievers," he wrote, "to prevent them from hindering the faith of Christ."[9]

U.S. HISTORY

As much as any society and more than many the United States has been dominated by the War Myth, often in its crusade form. In colonial times the puritan preacher Cotton Mather labeled native Americans as "a treacherous and barbarous enemy." He summoned the colonists to go forth against "Amalek annoying this Israel in the wilderness."[10] Just as the Israel of old conquered those Amalekites who stood in their way, God would help the new Israel overcome by the sword their current barbarous enemy.

During the Pequot War in 1637 several hundred native Americans were killed in one bloody confrontation. The colonial minister Thomas Shepard described the event as guided by "the Providence of God," and called the massacre a "divine slaughter."[11] The best way to deal with these problem people is to suppress them. God wants it that way.

Settlers moved out of their early eastern enclaves toward the frontier in search of a better life. The religious among them were encouraged by the Biblical command to "be fruitful and increase in number; fill the earth and subdue it" (Genesis 1:28).

This meant, most felt, subduing, in addition to the earth, all native peoples who opposed them.

Later most Americans, whether they knew it by its proper name or not, accepted the theory of Social Darwinism, that in human society as well as the animal kingdom survival goes to the fittest. And so does success. "Nice guys finish last," in the immortal words of baseball manager Leo Durocher. Those people who met the challenges, overcame the hardships, won the battles, were thought to be a better breed. Those who didn't were losers, and considered inferior. If you were able to beat down the challengers and get ahead of the pack, you must be stronger, worthier. If you didn't stand and fight, or if you did and you didn't win, you were thought to be weak, unworthy, a wimp.

U.S. policy toward Latin America has been dominated by the War Myth. The Monroe Doctrine in 1823 declared that the hemisphere was a North American preserve, and warned European powers away. Those people down there needed our energy and our enterprise, ran the assumption. They tend to be lazy, but we can put them to work. And they can learn by our example. Latin America is our backyard. We don't want any European powers meddling in it. U.S. business and industry expanded extensively in the late nineteenth and early twentieth centuries. President Theodore Roosevelt announced in 1904 that the U.S. had the right to "exercise international police power" to prevent "chronic wrong-doing" in the western hemisphere.[12] The chronic wrong-doing was perpetuated, in his eyes, by those inferior, illiterate, indolent people south of the border who didn't appreciate our way of doing business. In the decades that followed, U.S. military intervention frequently put down indigenous uprisings that threatened American interests.

The U.S. entered both world wars in the aura of a crusade. Churchgoers in Washington, D.C., heard it called that in a sermon at the height of World War I: "It is God who has summoned us to this war . . . This conflict is indeed a crusade, the greatest in history, the holiest. It is in the profoundest and truest sense a Holy War . . . Yes, it is Christ, the King of Righteousness, who calls us to grapple in deadly strife with this unholy and blasphemous power.[13] President Franklin Roosevelt invoked God to help in the all-out war effort he announced after Pearl Harbor: "No matter how long it may take us to overcome this premeditated invasion, the American people, in their righteous might, will win through to absolute victory . . . With confidence in our armed forces, with the unbounded determination of our people, we will gain the inevitable triumph. So help us God." General Dwight Eisenhower entitled his war memoirs *Crusade in Europe*, expressing the feelings of most Americans toward the war.

The War Myth continues to have deep roots in our culture. People who advocate the death penalty as a deterrent to murder are under its influence. So are those who believe that beefing up police forces is the best way to cope with crime. Because fear of punishment often inhibits unruly behavior, the War Myth has a firm grounding in reality. But human nature is complex enough that the opposite approach also has considerable appeal.

THE PEACE MYTH

The Bible contains not only war myths, but also the basic Peace Myth: God loves the stranger, the potential enemy; God's people should also. "Yahweh your God is God of gods and Lord of Lords . . . It is he who sees justice done for the orphan and widow, who loves the stranger and gives him food and clothing. Love the stranger, then, for you were strangers in the land of Egypt" (Deuteronomy 10:17-19).[14] We should approach people who are different not in fear, which leads to defensiveness and often results in hostility. The basic attitude is not to be hostility, but hospitality. We should provide strangers with food and clothing. Reach out to them as human beings. Remember how you felt when you were strangers yourselves in the land of Egypt, the command goes. They're isolated and afraid, just like you were. Go beyond appearances, relate to them as people, people in distress. God gives the example. You should follow it.

The Peace Myth is embodied in another important

Biblical image, the peaceful intermingling of otherwise incom-
patible creatures in the age of the Messiah (Isaiah 11:6-8):

> The wolf will live with the lamb,
>> the leopard will lie down with the goat,
> the calf and the lion and the yearling together;
>> and a little child will lead them.
> The cow will feed with the bear,
>> their young will lie down together,
>> and the lion will eat straw like the ox.
> The infant will play near the hole of the cobra,
>> and the young child put his hand into the viper's nest.
>> (Isaiah 11:6-8).

The antipathetic pairs getting along with each other symbolize
antagonistic people living together in harmony, in Messianic
times. The Peace Myth holds out the ideal of *shalom*. People,
no matter how difficult things may be between them, can go
beyond their differences and live together in a sufficient degree
of harmony.

According to the prophet Micah, this harmony will
come about through obeying God's law (Micah 4:2-3):

> The law will go out from Zion,
>> the word of the Lord from Jerusalem.
> He will judge between many peoples
>> and will settle disputes for strong nations far and wide.
> They will beat their swords into plowshares
>> and their spears into pruning hooks.
> Nation will not take up sword against nation,
>> nor will they train for war anymore.

In Biblical times the Peace Myth coexisted uneasily with the
War Myth. While prophets emphasized the former, people
tended to live by the latter. When the Babylonians attacked
Jerusalem, its citizens gathered their resources to defend themselves. Jewish authorities hoped that an alliance with Egypt
would bring rescuing troops to their aid. The War Myth was
in command. But the prophet Jeremiah saw that these prepara-
tions were futile. Jerusalem could be saved only by following

the ways of God. He had confidence that if the nation returned
to justice and honesty, God would somehow save them. If not,
they would be defeated. His message to King Zedekiah was
in the spirit of the Peace Myth (Jeremiah 22:3-5).

> This is what the Lord says: Do what is just and right.
> Rescue from the hand of his oppressor the one who has
> been robbed. Do no wrong or violence to the alien, the
> fatherless or the widow, and do not shed innocent blood
> in this place. For if you are careful to carry out these com-
> mands, then kings who sit on David's throne will come
> through the gates of this palace . . . But if you do not
> obey these commands, declares the Lord, I swear by
> myself that this palace will become a ruin.

Instead of concentrating on military defense, concentrate on
keeping God's law. Treat your people fairly, that's what God
wants. Then you will weather this storm, and your successor
kings will follow you in living in this palace. King Zedekiah
wavered. He respected Jeremiah. But the influence of the War
Myth was too strong. He ordered Jeremiah imprisoned, then
reinforced the defenses. But to no avail. Jeremiah had been
right. The Babylonians broke through and conquered.
    Jesus constantly advocated conduct based on the Peace
Myth. In one passage in the Sermon on the Mount (Matthew
5:38-39, 43-44) he explicitly contrasted it with the War Myth.

> You have heard that it was said, "Eye for eye, and tooth
> for tooth." But I tell you, do not resist an evil person.
> If someone strikes you on the right cheek, turn to him
> the other also . . . You have heard that it was said, "Love
> your neighbor and hate your enemy." But I tell you, Love
> your enemies and pray for those who persecute you.

Turning the other cheek and loving one's enemies are prototypical expressions of the Peace Myth in action. When someone
attacks you, absorb the blows initially. Don't fight back and
escalate the conflict. Approach the attacker with love. Jesus
saw a dismal future for those who took guidance from the War

Myth. When Peter tried to defend him in the Garden of Geth-semane he observed, "All who draw the sword will die by the sword" (Matthew 26:51).

The Peace Myth is based on the belief that life provides a great opportunity for positive human interaction. We can bring out the best in each other. The Peace Myth acknowledges human weaknesses and recognizes that people sometimes take advantage of others. But our reaction should be as nonviolent as posible. People will usually do what is right if given suffi-cient chance. They, we all, need to be encouraged more than coerced. Our potential for destruction can be defused, or channeled into helpful human endeavors, if we have a mind to do so.

The ancient Chinese symbol of Yin and Yang expressed the ideal harmony envisioned in the Peace Myth. The world, human as well as natural, is an interplay of forces: masculine-feminine, hot-cold, wet-dry. The best configuration is not the assertion of one at the expense of the others, but the delicate interweaving of both. The Chinese philosopher Lao Tzu, six centuries before Christ, applied this understanding to human conflict: actively foster the harmony in human relationships. When the harmony is interrupted, try to put it back. He ex-pressed it this way: "To those who are good to me I am good; and to those who are not good to me, I am also good;—and thus all get to be good. To those who are sincere with me, I am sincere; and to those who are not sincere with me, I am also sincere;—and thus all get to be sincere."[15]

The same ideal of conduct is found in another ancient culture, India. There it was best expressed in the Hindu religious classic *Bhagavad-Gita*, the Song of God. One of the most im-portant Hindu deities is portrayed as saying: "A man should not hate any living creature. Let him be friendly and compas-sionate to all. He must free himself from the delusion of 'I' and 'mine.' He must be forgiving, ever-contented, self-controlled, united constantly with me in meditation."[16] Gandhi, whose life was a shining expression of the Peace Myth, testified that he gained great comfort and courage from the *Bhagavad-Gita.*

CHRISTIAN EXPERIENCE

The earliest generations of Christians sensed the different directions pointed to by the War and Peace Myths. Most were clear about the course their lives should take, in the spirit of their Lord, Jesus. "The Lord, in disarming Peter, ungirded every soldier," wrote the third century theologian Tertullian. When Jesus told Peter to put his sword away, he meant to disarm all people, including those who were professionally pursuing the path of the War Myth. "We, who used to kill one another, do not make war on our enemies," said another Church Father, Justin. Before we became Christians we tolerated, or even reveled in, violence, hurting others. But no more. We don't even believe in war against our enemies. Kill us if you must. We won't fight back. We don't believe in it any more. These early Christians would rather die as martyrs than live as fighters.

In subsequent centuries the Peace Myth survived in Christendom primarily in monasteries. But some lived it outside, in the world. Peter Waldo and a group of dedicated people in Lyons, France, around 1170, modeled their lifestyle on the Sermon on the Mount. They repudiated oaths, capital punishment, all shedding of blood, and military service. The authorities at first harassed them, then threatened them with death if they continued living and talking in this absurd way. Many sought safety in the Alps. Today the Waldensian Church in northern Italy bears testimony to the ideals that animated Peter Waldo eight centuries ago.

In the early 1200s Francis of Assisi stood out as a person much like Waldo. Francis forbade his followers to bear arms, especially in the Crusades. Francis himself, according to one legend, traveled to the camp of the Sultan of Babylon in an effort to convert him to Christ. Such a conversion would have eliminated the very need for a Crusade, Francis thought. He was allowed to pass unharmed through the ranks of the soldiers on both sides. His personal courage impressed everyone, even the Sultan who, although he did not convert, did receive Francis, listened to him, and let him leave alive—to the amazement of the armed bystanders.

The followers of John Wycliff, basing their stand squarely on the Gospel, urged the English parliament in 1395 to condemn war and all manslaughter. Parliament, of course, refused. Wycliff had to face religious as well as civil rejection for his socially unorthodox position. Some of his writings reached Bohemia, where they were taken up by John Hus in his preaching at the University of Prague. Unfortunately Hus also met the fate of many who dissent from the mainstream in the name of peace. He was burned at the stake during the Council of Constance in 1415.

Although the United States, as many other cultures, is predominantly influenced by the War Myth, the Peace Myth has been present also, if with considerably less acclaim. The Quaker William Penn concluded a peace treaty with the Delaware Indians who lived in his proprietary land now known as Pennsylvania. The treaty specified that the doors of the settlers' homes would always be open to the Indians, and the homes of the Indians would always be open to the settlers. They should welcome each other as neighbors. That agreement preserved peace in Pennsylvania for half a century. When warfare broke out between the native Americans and the colonists, as it did in other parts of the soon-to-be United States in the 1750s, the Delawares spared the lives of the Quaker families who had lived by Penn's treaty.

In every one of America's wars a handful of courageous young men refused to participate, in the conviction that killing was not the right way to settle differences. Conscientious objectors, especially from the Mennonites, Quakers, and the Moravian Brethren—the three Christian bodies called the Historic Peace Churches—gave quiet witness to another way than war of meeting the nation's challenges. The U.S. Catholic bishops, in *The Challenge of Peace*, their 1983 Pastoral Letter on War and Peace, called such men "deeply sincere individuals who, far from being indifferent or apathetic to world evils, believe strongly in conscience that they are but defending true peace by refusing to bear arms."[17]

The Peace Myth is reflected in Father Flanagan's motto, "There's no such thing as a bad boy," which led him to found the acclaimed Boys Town in Nebraska. It inspired Grantland Rice's sports ideal, "It's not whether you've won or lost, it's how you played the game." It influenced the movements for abolition of slavery, women's suffrage, civil rights, and peace during the Vietnam years. It can be felt today in the nuclear freeze campaign, in opposition to capital punishment, and in all movements for peaceful solutions to conflict.

THE KINGDOM OF HEAVEN

The clearest Biblical expression of the Peace Myth is the Kingdom of Heaven. The eminent Dutch theologian Edward Schillebeeckx called it one of "the great metaphorical master images" in human language. The Kingdom is the central focus of Jesus' teaching in the synoptic gospels. The Kingdom in its fulness means, in Schillebeeckx's words, "the final liberation and salvation of the peaceful community of all human beings."[18] We are painfully conscious that we are at the moment not fully liberated. We are not fully saved. Our communities are not fully peaceful. But we long for that condition down the road where all these defects will be remedied. We want people freed from poverty, sickness, ignorance, hatred, oppression. We want the goods of the earth shared more equitably.

All this is promised in the image of the Kingdom. It's the ideal existence, the goal up ahead we would like to see fulfilled even when we know it's beyond our human means to fulfill it. So we pray that the Kingdom may come, that God's will be done on earth as it is in heaven. The Kingdom is like the impossible dream. Except that it's not completely impossible. Despite the daily difficulties that weigh us down, despite the underlying hardness of governments insensitive to human needs, despite the outbreak of random violence, we catch a glimpse of the goodness that transforms, of kindness that cuts through barriers.

The New Testament teaches that the Kingdom of Heaven has already begun in the person of Jesus. God's reign, where the lion will lie down with the lamb, where people will not train for war any more, began to break in on human life with Jesus. His words and actions started a new and decisive phase of God's reign in this world. With Jesus the emphasis is more on earth than on heaven, on this life more than the afterlife, on human beings more than heavenly beings. At the beginning of his ministry Jesus went into the synagogue in his home town of Nazareth. During a Sabbath service he read from the scroll of Isaiah: "The Spirit of the Lord is on me, because he has anointed me to preach good news to the poor. He has sent me to proclaim freedom for the prisoners, and recovery of sight for the blind, to release the oppressed, to proclaim the year of the Lord's favor." Then he said, "Today this scripture is fulfilled in your hearing" (Luke 4:18-19, 21). Jesus spent the rest of his life taking up these very earthly tasks.

When John the Baptist sent his disciples to ask if Jesus was indeed the one they were waiting for, he answered, "Go back and report to John what you hear and see. The blind receive sight, the lame walk, those who have leprosy are cured, the deaf hear, the dead are raised up and the good news is preached to the poor" (Matthew 11:4-5). The Kingdom of Heaven has a definite earthly component. When Jesus said that his Kingdom was not of this world, he meant that it was not of the world of the War Myth. His Kingdom was not of the world of domination, of winning through intimidation. "You know that those who are regarded as rulers of the Gentiles lord it over them, and their high officials exercise authority over them. Not so with you. Instead, whoever wants to become great among you must be your servant, and whoever wants to be first must be slave of all" (Mark 10:42-4).

Jesus led the way in the earthly phase of the Kingdom by being a super servant: healing the sick, giving sight to the blind and hearing to the deaf, bringing good news to the poor.

By involving all his followers in similar actions of healing and helping, he insured that his efforts would be carried forward as long as the Christian faith lived. He elevated love of neighbor to the same level as love of God. The first commandment, he said, is "Love the Lord your God with all your heart" (Matthew 22:37). "And the second is like it"—like it in importance—"Love your neighbor as yourself" (Matthew 22:39). Through the parable of the Good Samaritan (Luke 10:25-37) he taught that our neighbor was anyone in need. Through the parable of the sheep and the goats at the last judgment (Matthew 25:31-46) he taught that eternal salvation depends on feeding the hungry, clothing the naked, and visiting prisoners.

The First Letter of John presented the same emphasis: "Anyone who does not love his brother, whom he has seen, cannot love God, whom he has not seen. And he has given us this command: Whoever loves God must also love his brother" (I John 4:20-21). The litmus test for being right with God is whether or not we love our neighbor. Paul said that all commandments "are summed up in this one rule: 'Love your neighbor as yourself'" (Romans 13:9). The Letter of James called it "the royal law found in Scripture" (James 2:8).

The Kingdom of Heaven is at hand in Jesus in two essential ways. First, he is the model of humanity and humaneness. He taught us what true human decency looks like. Secondly, he encouraged his followers of all centuries to improve the lot of other human beings. Jesus' program during the short years he lived in this world has been aptly summed up by the Swiss theologian Hans King as human liberation and salvation.[19] Jesus wanted to free people from anything that restrained them from developing their best potential. He wanted to show them the way to the final fulfillment of God's kingdom.

CONVERSION

Although the culminaton of God's Kingdom is beyond our control, here and there we can do something to help its progress. We can build bits and pieces of the Kingdom. We can establish elements of it. God's kingdom will never be on earth in its perfection, but we can try to act according to it in our own personal relationships. And because the Kingdom of Heaven is different from the prevailing climate in most of the cultures that make up the present map of the world, to follow the way of the Kingdom means to shift our perspective, to change our way of thinking.

In the context of enemies we see that we have a choice. Toward every enemy we can react in the culturally acknowledged ways of flight or fight, or the Kingdom way of positive love. But, as Scripture scholar Father Donald Senior has said, Jesus' teaching compels us to live according to the future we most desire to see. And the future we most desire is the Kingdom. Practically, this means turning from the War Myth to the Peace Myth. Instead of allowing our lives to be dominated by the belief that others have aggressive designs and that survival necessitates counterhostility, we can choose to believe that everyone is essentially decent and wants to love.

A change in outlook of this dimension is expressed in the Greek word *metanoia:* change of mind, usually translated in the Gospels as "repent." It's necessary for the coming Kingdom. "Jesus went into Galilee, proclaiming the good news of God. 'The time has come,' he said. 'The Kingdom of God is near. Repent and believe the good news!'" (Mark 1:14-15). The good news is the approach of the Kingdom. It calls us to a whole new way of looking at human affairs. Belief—personal acceptance of this good news—is more than intellectual assent, more than understanding the formula. It involves significant changes of attitude, that mental and emotional turnabout called conversion.

Which of the two myths, which of the two mentalities, is dominant in our lives is beyond our control—until we're aware that we have a choice. We are not prisoners of our past. We have a measure of freedom that allows us to move in another direction. We can remove ourselves from the pressures of our former way of looking at the world, and take up another way of seeing things.

Some who like to call themselves realists assert that survival has been the fortune of those who followed the War Myth. They say that tribes and peoples who lived by the Peace Myth were eventually destroyed by enemies they were incapable of resisting.[20] But the opposite is closer to the truth. People have survived despite following the War Myth. Anthropologist Ashley Montagu has written that cooperation, not competition, is the dominant principle of life: "Throughout the five million years or so of man's evolution the highest premium has been placed on cooperation . . . or else there would be no human beings today."[21] The War Myth and the war mentality have created far more havoc and made life far more punishing then it need be.

But whatever the verdict about the past, the future absolutely depends on switching to the Peace Myth. Maybe it has taken nuclear weapons to demonstrate the inadequacy of the War Myth conclusively, just as Auschwitz revealed the horrendous implications of racism. Gandhi once said, "An eye for an eye leaves everyone blind." In the nuclear age it will leave everyone dead.

Those who see the possibility of changing must do it— and can do it—without waiting for others to make the switch. When we say we'll change only when our enemies do, we're in for a long wait. But when we change first, we can begin to make good things happen. It's not an easy switch to make. It involves more than a new insight, more than a shift of mental perspective. It involves the depths of one's personality, what Charny calls "the ever-present, purposeful, pulsating energy or strength for being which charges the very spirit."[22] It involves a reorientation of our life-force, a change in the way we comport ourselves in relation to the world around us. When we make the change, we link ourselves with the great turning around of the world from the course of nuclear destruction to the way of peace. Our individual effort to live by the Peace Myth has worldwide ramifications. We become part of a great movement spreading across the globe that says, in the stirring words of Pope Paul VI to the United Nations, "No more war, war never again. Peace, it is peace which must guide the destinies of peoples and of all humankind."

When we make the switch from the War Myth to the Peace Myth we follow the call of the Second Vatican Council to evaluate war with an entirely new attitude. Pope John Paul II said, during his 1981 visit to Hiroshima, "From now on it is only through a conscious choice and through a deliberate policy that humanity can survive." He saw that the very survival of the human race depends on our making a "conscious choice," and then setting forth the public policies that can implement the choice. The U.S. Catholic bishops, in their Peace Pastoral, emphasized our responsibility to make that choice: "We have grave human, moral and political responsibilities to see that a 'conscious choice' is made to save humanity."[23] Although neither the Pope nor the U.S. bishops identified that choice with a total repudiation of violence toward enemies, it seems clear that their words pointed in that direction. If we choose to set out on that journey we can find encouragement in the way Jesus responded to his own enemies.

DISCUSSION QUESTIONS

1. Where do you see the War Myth reflected in life today—television, politics, advertising?

2. Where do you see the Peace Myth today?

3. Is the crusade mentality still around? Where is it likely to show up most prominently?

4. Which of the two, the War Myth or the Peace Myth, do you think better represents the reality of interpersonal interaction as you have experienced it?

5. If one wanted to become more absorbed in the Peace Myth, what resources—people, places, literature— might be helpful?

CHAPTER THREE

JESUS AND HIS ENEMIES

During the three years Jesus walked the rocky roads of Galilee and made his presence felt in Jerusalem, he accumulated an impressive array of enemies. Some of them finally killed him: the Roman governor who sentenced him to death, and the Roman soldiers who crucified him. But almost from the beginning of his public life people were out to get him. In the third chapter of Mark's Gospel we read of a confrontation between Jesus and some Pharisees. When it was over, "the Pharisees went out and began to plot with the Herodians how they might kill Jesus" (Mark 3:6). Those Pharisees and Herodians join the Roman officials on the list of his enemies.

So do the "chief priests and teachers of the law"(Scribes)

who were "looking for a way to kill him" (Mark 11:18). Jesus' enemies also include Herod Antipas, tetrarch of Galilee: "Some Pharisees came to Jesus and said to him, 'leave this place and go somewhere else. Herod wants to kill you'" (Luke 13:31); and the council of Jewish officials, the Sanhedrin, who set in motion the chain of events which resulted in his death. "One of them . . . spoke up, 'You know nothing at all! You do not realize that it is better for you that one man die for the people than that the whole nation perish . . . So from that day on they plotted to take his life" (John 11:49,53).

Quickly other enemies emerged: Judas, who betrayed him; the high priest who led the Sanhedrin in convicting him of blasphemy and turning him over to the Romans; finally Pontius Pilate, who signed his death warrant, and the professional executioners who mocked him and beat him and nailed him to the cross. As we try to understand why each of these enemies wanted to hurt Jesus, we will also be attentive to the ways he responded to them.

THE ENEMIES

The Romans   Long before they focused consciously on Jesus, the Roman authorities were his enemies to the extent that they were enemies of all the oppressed people of the land of Israel, the territory they called Palestine. Rome had taken control of it in 63 B.C. as part of its expanding empire.

The Roman occupation of Palestine was not a pretty affair. They ruled by force and the threat of force. They tortured to death any rebels they captured. They forced people at sword point to carry military baggage. They garrisoned soldiers at conspicuous sites: in Capernaum by the Lake, in Sepphoris near Nazareth, in Jerusalem by the Temple, in Caesarea, their headquarters on the coast. The Romans were prime examples of the War Myth in action. Their Pax Romana operated on the principle of peace through strength. Roman violence was never far beneath the surface in the Holy Land of Jesus' day.

Empire, then and now, exists primarily for power and

profit. Those who control it might make lofty claims of bringing civilization, or promoting peace, or establishing law and
order. They may insist they are enhancing life for the natives
by preaching the true religion, spreading democracy, or ad-
vancing the cause of socialism. But the principal payoffs are
the satisfaction they get from dominating others, and their personal enrichment at the expense of the subservient populations.

The Romans had an overwhelming sense of superiority.
They were proud of their generosity in allowing inferior people
to participate in their great enterprise. If asked why they were
in Spain or Africa or Greece or Palestine, they would have
answered that they offered their subjects something far better
than independence: the opportunity of sharing in the magnifi-
cence of the Empire itself. They expected to be treated everywhere as the master race they were confident they were.[1]

What the Romans wanted from Palestine was territory
and tribute. For strategic purposes they needed to control that
small strip of land which for centuries had been the passage-
way between Africa and Asia. They also wanted money. The
expenses of empire were great. Palestine was not a source of
other assets, like Egypt for ivory, Cappadocia for horses, Spain
for silver and tin. But even from poor provinces like Palestine
they could get revenue. The Romans farmed out the collection of taxes to commercial companies. These in turn employed
a large number of strong-armed men called publicans, whose
job was to come up with the taxes by any means they deemed
necessary. If they collected more than their quota they could
keep the surplus, no questions asked. Provinces were expected
to collect enough to pay for their own administration, and to
insure a constant flow of money to Rome. The whole process,
backed up by the army, was administered by a governor.

Many governors were procurators, men with prior experience in Roman financial affairs. Few were honest, like
Cicero, or Pliny the Younger. Most were interested in money
not only for the Empire, but also for themselves. During their
tour of duty they followed the unwritten custom to accumu-
late as much as the traffic would bear. In Palestine, one effective
method was to taunt the people by displaying the Roman eagle,
a graven image abhorrent to the Jews. Those provoked into

protesting were imprisoned or killed, their property confiscated for the governor's private coffers. In Roman imperial circles this was one of the fringe benefits of the job.

Palestine was a typical province, except that its people were somewhat more pesky. Military pressure had to be tight. The Romans were alert for signs of rebellion. They squelched it quickly and ruthlessly.

Pharisees and Scribes   Although a few Jewish people collaborated with the Romans, most disliked them severely. Reaction took different forms. Some pious Jews, Zealots, went the route of armed resistance. They believed the only good Roman was a dead Roman. Other devout believers repudiated political action and concentrated on living as closely as they could by the Law of Moses, their revered Torah. They had come, over the past several centuries of Greek and Roman domination, to be called by the Hebrew word *p'rushim*, Pharisees, meaning "separated ones." Their approach was, as Temple University professor Gerard Sloyan characterized it, "the one Jeremiah had counseled centuries before in the face of the Assyrian threat. The Pharisees favored letting history take its course while they placed all their trust in the Lord. He would protect them."[2] The Pharisees were more interested in religious righteousness than in national liberation.

They were not content with superficial observance or half-hearted compliance with the Torah. They believed that God had given an oral Law, an unwritten Torah, which complemented and clarified the written one. This combination, they felt, represented God's will for the Chosen People. In their pursuit of that ritual purity they deemed devotion, some of them adopted a posture of rigid religiosity, basing life on the minutiae of the Law rather than on the spirit behind it.

At the time of Jesus the Pharisees were loosely organized in what is often called a "party." They were a sect within the Judaism of their day. Some Pharisees, respected for their expertise in the Law, were called on to apply it to religious and secular questions. These were the Scribes, in effect religious lawyers. Judaism had a long tradition of Scribes. But in Jesus' time most Scribes were Pharisees. The Gospels usually link them together.

Pharisees who met Jesus reacted to him in different ways. Some tried to help him, warning him about Herod and advising him to leave Galilee for his own safety (Luke 13:31). The Pharisee Nicodemus came to him at night for instruction (John 3:1). At least one Pharisee invited Jesus to his home for dinner (Luke 7:36). But others, according to the Gospels, disliked him to the point of wanting to kill him.

Theirs was a strong reaction. Scripture scholar John McKenzie suggests that it may have been because Jesus threatened their position as religious leaders.[3] His charismatic ways were eroding their prominence as paragons of piety. Many Jews had begun looking to Jesus instead of to the Pharisees for guidance in the Law. Jesus had suggested that religous practices be put in a broader perspective. They should serve true human good, not be rigidly obeyed for their own sakes. Follow the Law, yes, but make exceptions in the interest of people's genuine needs. Pick the grain on the Sabbath, if you need it because you're hungry. The Sabbath was made for people, not people for the Sabbath (Mark 2:27). Leave your gift in front of the altar, go and be reconciled with your brother or sister, then come back and offer your gift (Matthew 5:24). Paul, who himself had been raised a Pharisee, expressed the same approach when he wrote that "the letter kills, but the Spirit gives life" (II Corinthians 3:6).

Many Pharisees sincerely tried to live up to the letter of the Law. But others did not, giving it lip service only. These Jesus called "hypocrites," the Greek word for actors on stage (Matthew 13:13). He told the people, "Do everything they tell you. But do not do what they do, for they do not practice what they preach" (Matthew 23:3). He confronted them openly, publicly, fearlessly. He argued with them about the influence of the Devil (Matthew 12:24-29). He challenged their religious legalism (Mark 7:5-13). And in an unparalleled series of castigations he hurled woe after woe at them, calling them "blind guides" (Matthew 23:16), "snakes," "brood of vipers" (Matthew 23:33).

Jesus wanted to jolt the Pharisees into a sense of proportionality about the Law they so revered. Confrontation is an established technique for changing attitudes. People sometimes see things differently when they are forced to face an opposing view. Jesus may well have been showing his love for these religiously sincere people, hoping that they would develop what he considered a more wholesome attitude toward the Law, as Paul later did. But Jesus' criticism stung. The hypocrites among them may have hated him enough for his rebukes that they wanted to kill him. Jesus' flexible approach to the whole body of ritual regulations was threatening to those who staked their lives on it. People who find security in a rigid framework of beliefs and practices sense inner chaos when that framework is challenged. They react defensively. In terms of enemy dynamics these Pharisees saw Jesus as dangerous. They felt vulnerable to him. They identified him as their enemy, so in self-defense they became his enemy. Rather than moving in the direction of the greater religious integrity Jesus advocated, they decided instead to silence him. At a time when the occupying Romans rested their rule on the constant threat of violence, death was taken for granted as a quick solution to a problem. The War Myth was in firm control, in Jewish as well as Roman circles. It makes sense, in this climate, that some Pharisees "plotted how they might kill Jesus" (Matthew 12:14).

But there's more to the story of this portrayal of Pharisees as Jesus' mortal enemies. When the Synoptic Gospels came to be written, some thirty-five to fifty years after the events they described took place, the Christian experience was well on its way. At that time the early Christian community found itself in significant struggle with leaders of the Jewish people. After the Romans destroyed the Jerusalem Temple in A.D. 70, Jewish authorities zealously concentrated on the other great symbol of their faith, the Law. They resented those Nazareans, followers of the Way, who believed that their Jesus had fulfilled the Law and ushered in the Reign of God. The Gospel of Matthew, particularly, was written in the urgency of that conflict. Matthew's focusing on the Pharisees and Scribes as Jesus' major enemies mirrors the tensions between the young Christian church and those Jews who felt that their survival depended on preserving their traditional ways. Matthew's portrayal of the hostility between Jesus and the Pharisees was colored by "the fact that Matthew remembers the controversies of Jesus' ministry from the perspective of the bitter struggle of his own day," as religious educators Robert Obach and Albert Kirk have duly noted.[4] Matthew wanted to convey to his readers that they need not feel oppressed by the attacks they were experiencing, as Jesus was not oppressed by the Pharisees' oppositon during his lifetime. In describing how Jesus stood up to them so clearly and so successfully, Matthew implies that fifty years later his Christian readers ought to do the same.

Those early controversies have long faded into history. But the Pharisees have become, wherever the New Testament is read, symbols of religious hypocrisy. The real Pharisees, whose spiritual descendants wrote the Talmud and kept the flame of Jewish faith alive through times of terrible trouble, had much in common with Jesus: respect for God's Law, religious seriousness, and a sense of the relative triviality of earthly affairs compared to the awesome ways of God. As Sloyan notes, Jesus "had no difficulty whatever with the genuine article, the sage who sought holiness in observance of the Law. He was an opponent of the counterfeit types . . . Unfortunately his reported teaching has kept the latter stereotype alive while not providing an equally vivid picture of the Separated who are such out of love."[5]

Herodians and Herod Antipas   If the Pharisees were motivated by religious purity, other enemies of Jesus were driven by political expediency. The Gospels mention a group called Herodians. Each time they are linked with the Pharisees as opponents of Jesus.[6] Most probably they were supporters of the rule of Herod and the Romans who backed it. Their allegiance was with Herod and his Roman masters.

After Herod the Great died in 4 B.C. the Romans divided the territory he had ruled as their agent. One of his sons, Archelaus, got the biggest part, including Judea and Samaria. He governed for nine years, but so inadequately that he had to be replaced by direct Roman administration. Another son, Philip, was given some scattered, sparsely settled territories in the northeast. A third son, Herod Antipas, obtained Perea across the Jordan, and the rolling hills and fertile farmland which was Galilee. Herodians were part of his entourage, household hangers-on.

The emperor Augustus had refused to designate Antipas as king, settling instead for the lesser title of tetrarch, ruler of a fourth part. Herod Antipas played the role of puppet to the hilt. He spied on other Roman operatives in the area. He courted favor with Augustus' successor, Tiberius, by naming the city he had built for his residence on the western shore of the Sea of Galilee after him. Antipas proved to be a survivor, maneuvering successfully for forty years under three emperors.

He devoted considerable energy not only to pleasing the Romans, but also to having a good time for himself. When he tired of his first wife he let her go and married a woman named Herodias, the divorced wife of his deceased half-brother. Although divorce was acceptable in Jewish life, marrying the wife of one's brother was not. John the Baptist protested this flagrant violation of Jewish law. Antipas had him arrested. Then, during one of the many banquets he threw for prominent Galileeans, he acceded to the request of Herodias' dancing daughter and ordered his executioner to cut off John's head.

It was this Herod Antipas who reportedly wanted to kill Jesus—not for any great reasons of state, but because Jesus, too, posed a threat to his marital life. Jesus had denounced divorce: "Anyone who divorces his wife, except for marital unfaithfulness, causes her to commit adultery, and anyone who marries a woman so divorced commits adultery" (Matthew 5:32). Antipas was so obsessed with public denunciations of his personal life and, perhaps, guilt over his capricious killing of the Baptist, that he imagined Jesus to be John come again to haunt him. "John, the man I beheaded, has been raised from the dead" (Mark 6:16). His Herodian minions joined with some of the Pharisees to see that their master's wish was carried out.

Jesus was not in the least intimidated by Herod's threat. "Go tell that fox," he said, that "I will drive out demons and heal people today and tomorrow, and on the third day I will reach my goal" (Luke 13:33). He continued to teach and preach and heal openly, in defiance of Herod and his henchmen.

Herod Antipas prospered under Roman patronage for a few more years. His big mistake came in A.D. 39 when he went to Rome at the insistence of his wife to ask the next Caesar, Caligula, to change his title from tetrarch to king. Instead, that erratic emperor exiled him to France. Antipas was heard from no more. Before his ambition got the best of him, he had met Jesus face-to-face for the only time, as far as we know, at Jesus' trial. That trial was engineered by other enemies of Jesus.

Chief Priests and the Sanhedrin   The large, imposing temple in Jerusalem was the physical center of Jewish religion and the cultural center of Jewish society. A corps of maintenance people—suppliers, bookkeepers, musicians, artisans, ritual functionaries of all kinds—kept the operations of the temple running as smoothly as possible. These were led by priests, whose positions were hereditary, passed down from generation to generation. The priests were organized hierarchically. Those at the top, who set the schedule of work for the rest and who controlled the treasury, held the rank of chief priest.

Some chief priests were also members of the Sanhedrin, the body of six dozen Jewish men to whom the Romans delegated matters of religious law and day-to-day administration. Besides the chief priests, the Sanhedrin also included elders from the leading families, and lawyer-scribes. Some of the Sanhedrin's chief priests and elders belonged to a party called Sadducees. This sect generally numbered among its members the wealthy elite of Jewish society. Religiously, they tended to a conservative view of the Law. They acknowledged only the written Torah, unlike the Pharisees, who accepted an oral tradition as well. Also unlike the Pharisees, who were isolationists, they tended to collaborate easily with the Romans.

The Sanhedrin was essentially a Roman tool. Jewish scholar Leo Trepp suggests that the Jewish people had two Sanhedrins during the time of Roman occupation, one for religious matters, the other for political affairs:"The Sanhedrin for religious matters was composed of scholars, met at appointed times, was bound by Jewish law, and therefore never sat at night, never handed down a conviction in criminal matters on the day of the trial, hence never held any trial sessions on the day before the Sabbath or any holiday. The other Sanhedrin was government appointed, composed of partisans of the Romans who were willing to give the semblance of legal sanction to acts of the Roman overlord."[7] If there were two, it was the second one that took an interest in Jesus.

One reason the Sanhedrin was hostile to Jesus arose from their unerring sense of Roman reaction. People were beginning to look on Jesus as the messiah. Here was potential for disaster. The Romans would not understand the subtleties of this title. They would consider a messiah to be an insurrectionist, bent on overthrowing Roman rule. The Romans who, as all empire builders, had a low threshold of tolerance for civil unrest, would lean heavily to extinguish rebellion, crushing whatever had to be crushed in the process. The Sanhedrin recognized this. "If we let him go on like this, everyone will believe in him, and then the Romans will come and take away both our place and our nation" (John 11:48).

Besides responsibility for their nation, many in the Sanhedrin must have felt a personal threat from Jesus. He was pulling the props out from under the entire social order over which they presided. They believed that the Jewish experience was inextricably linked to the temple and its ritual. Jesus downplayed the temple's importance. If that wasn't enough, his affirmation of the poor implied the injustice of the wealthy. His siding with sinners offended a deeply entrenched social prejudice. His respect for women threatened the bedrock patriarchy. His relegation of the family to a secondary place in the Kingdom of Heaven shook the foundations of their tribal society. Members of the Sanhedrin held their prestige precariously. They could lose it if large numbers of people started living according to Jesus' teaching, as surely as they could lose it if the Romans cracked down after Jesus became the occasion of widespread public unrest.

All of this is capsuled in Mark's cryptic statement, "The chief priests and teachers of the law . . . began looking for a way to kill him, for they feared him, because the whole crowd was amazed at his teaching" (Mark 11:18).

Unlike his attitude toward the Pharisees and Herod, Jesus reacted cautiously to the Sanhedrin. He took their threat very seriously. "Therefore Jesus no longer moved about publicly among them. Instead he withdrew to a region near the desert, to a village called Ephraim, where he stayed with his disciples" (John 11:54). His first response was evasion. Get away, hide from them. He was careful not to take unnecessary risks.

But he did not stay away from the action for long. He entered Jerusalem with some fanfare a few days before the Passover feast. There he preached boldly in public, despite the danger from the Sanhedrin. He appreciated the power of the crowds who surrounded him during the day. The authorities hesitated to seize him openly, "or there may be a riot among the people" (Matthew 26:5). Jesus banked on this protection. He took a calculated risk that he could escape arrest during the day. But he took precautions at night. "When he finished speaking, Jesus left and hid himself from them" (John 12:36). Luke specifies his hiding place during those tense days preceding the Passover. "Each day Jesus was teaching in the temple, and each evening he went out to spend the night on the hill called the Mount of Olives" (Luke 22:37).

Never, as far as we know, did he have any plans to defend himself physically. When he told his disciples, after their last supper together, "If you don't have a sword, sell your cloak and buy one" (Luke 22:36), he was speaking metaphorically. He wanted them to be mentally and spiritually prepared for the ordeal. But they took him literally. "See, Lord, here are two swords" (Luke 23:38). Rather than getting into a long discussion to explain what he meant, he simply replied, "That is enough" (Luke 22:38), meaning "Enough of this. Let's get going."[8]

His evasiveness frustrated the Sanhedrin. Hence the need for a betrayer, to lead them to where he was hiding out at night. They "had given orders that if anyone found out where Jesus was, he should report it so that they might arrest him (John 11:57).

Judas   Jesus' death was a certainty, given his continuing challenge of the authorities after they had decided he must be eliminated. It was only a matter of time when they would have found out where he was staying. Judas made things easier.

Judas is a fascinating figure—the betrayer, the friend turned enemy, the prototypical turncoat. The Gospels do not satisfy our curiosity. Even his name is ambiguous. Iscariot can mean a man from Kerioth, a town in the south of Judea— which would have made Judas the only certain non-Galilean member of the Twelve. Or it could come from the Latin *sicarius*, dagger-man, a word the Romans used for an armed revolutionary.

His motives in betraying Jesus were not clear, either. They may have been simple greed. But only Matthew portrays Judas as asking for a payment. "What are you willing to give me if I hand him over to you?" (Matthew 26:15). Mark says that Judas offered to betray Jesus first, and then "they promised to give him money" (Mark 14:13). Luke doesn't try to suggest a motive. He simply says that "Satan entered Judas," and then he "went to the chief priests and officers of the temple guard and discussed with them how he might betray Jesus" (Luke 22:3-4).

His motives may have been political. If he was a *sicarius*, he could have joined the Twelve, believing Jesus was the promised messiah who would lead a successful revolt to drive out the hated Romans. When he finally understood that Jesus' revolution was first spiritual and that no armed uprising was in the cards, Judas could have seen Jesus as a threat to the real messiah. If people followed Jesus in his way of personal regeneration, he might have thought, they would be in no mood to follow the true Messiah when he appeared to fight against the Romans. Jesus therefore had to be eliminated so that the revolution could go forward.

If this was in fact his motive, he would have been the only revolutionary known to be hostile to Jesus. There were many others around at the time, notably the Zealots. We might have assumed that the Zealots would also be Jesus' enemies, thinking he was holding back their revolution through moderation. But the Gospels give no hint of Zealot opposition. In fact, one of his twelve closest disciples, Simon, is identified as a Zealot (Mark 3:18).

Whatever Judas' reasons, he made his deal with the authorities. The Gospels indicate that Jesus knew about it, but did nothing to prevent the betrayal. His time had come, he must see it through to the end. He did, however, make sure Judas knew he was aware of what was going on. At the Last Supper he announced to his disciples, "One of you will betray me" (Matthew 26:21). Judas said, "Surely not I, Rabbi?" Jesus answered, "Yes, it is you" (Matthew 26:29). But he evidently spoke in a low tone so that the others did not hear.

Jesus appealed to Judas' conscience by impressing on him the ugly consequences of his act. "The Son of Man will go just as it is written about him. But woe to that man who betrays the Son of Man! It would be better for him if he had not been born" (Mark 14:21). Awesome words, but veiled from everyone except Judas. Quite possibly Jesus understood very well the human confusion out of which Judas was acting: a weak man succumbing to greed, or a zealous man overcome with misguided patriotism. Other disciples had their weaknesses, too. James and John, with Peter, would fall asleep in the garden when he needed their support. The others would desert him when he was arrested. Peter would deny him.

Although he spoke to Judas, he did nothing to embarrass him publicly, acting in the full spirit of the Peace Myth; he didn't give Judas the opportunity to become defensive and so reinforce his decision. Nor did he bring the others in on it at all. He quietly gave Judas the opportunity to change without having to back down in front of his colleagues. But Judas didn't change. So Jesus told him to get moving. "What you are about to do, do quickly" (John 13:27). The others thought Jesus was sending him on some errand "to buy what was needed for the Feast, or to give something to the poor" (John 13:29).

They had one last encounter. Judas brought the temple police to the place where Jesus was praying on the Mount of Olives. Even here he did not embarrass Judas, did not give any grounds for Judas' hostility, still called him "Friend" (Matthew 26:50). To the very end he was hoping that Judas would repent, as Peter later did, and be better for it.

Judas was, in fact, touched. Matthew says he was

"seized with remorse" (Matthew 27:3) when he saw that Jesus was condemned to death. After that we don't know what happened to him. The New Testament contains two conflicting stories about his end. Matthew says he returned the money, and "went away and hanged himself" (Matthew 27:5). According to the Acts of the Apostles Judas bought a field with the money, but then suffered some kind of accident: "There he fell headlong, his body burst open and all his intestines spilled out" (Acts 1:18).

At any rate Judas was a minor enemy compared to those authorities who wanted Jesus dead—and were in a position to see it done.

The High Priest   Each year the Romans appointed one of the chief priests to preside over the Sanhedrin. Known as the high priest, this favored friend of the Romans enjoyed considerable power and prestige in Jewish circles. Power is important enough to some people that they will sacrifice other values to attain it. Power to bend others to one's will, power to imprint one's personality on events, power to assert one's ego against opposition—this has always been one of life's enticing goals. For many it surpasses wealth and pleasure in desirability.

A man named Caiaphas was high priest during Jesus' time. He was a figurehead in the political machine operated by his father-in-law, Annas. The old man had been high priest himself from A.D. 6 to 15, then managed to have several of his sons named to the position. In A.D. 18 he tapped his son-in-law, Caiaphas, whom the Roman governor duly appointed. Caiaphas held the post for the next eighteen years, satisfying the whims of his father-in-law, and giving the Romans the legal nicety they wanted. Under his direction the Sanhedrin sent the temple guard to arrest Jesus.

Judas led these Roman soldiers and temple police to Jesus' hiding place in the olive grove of Gethsemane. Jesus allowed them to take him. He had no earthly escape. And he disavowed a heavenly one. "Do you think that I cannot call on my Father, and he will at once put at my disposal more than twelve legions of angels? But how then would the

Scriptures be fulfilled that say it must happen in this way?"
(Matthew 26:53-4).

Jesus realized that these agents of the Sanhedrin were
only instruments of others, doing the job for which they were
being paid. They did not bear the primary responsibility for
what was taking place. But his response was more than just
correct compliance. He let them know that what they were
doing was ill-advised. Carrying out orders to arrest him was
a mission of which they should not be proud. "Am I leading
a rebellion, that you have come with swords and clubs? Every
day I was with you in the temple courts, and you did not lay
a hand on me. But this is your hour—when darkness reigns"
(Luke 22:52-3). He treated them respectfully, but his respect
included letting them know the truth about what they were
doing. Only then did they take him bodily. "They bound him"
(John 18:12), and "took him into the house of the high priest"
(Luke 22:54).

Caiaphas was waiting for him. So was Annas, his mentor, and the rest of the Sanhedrin. Jesus did not show the same
respect for these men that he had shown to the arresting agents.
Before this Sanhedrin Jesus at first remained silent. He refused
to cooperate with them, refused to respond to the witnesses
they had procured, refused to lend dignity to this kangaroo
court. The high priest asked him, "Are you not going to
answer? What is this testimony that these men are bringing
against you?" (Mark 14:60). Jesus said nothing. He would not
enter into their illegal process. At one point he turned the
interrogation back on itself. "I have spoken openly to the
world," he said. "I always taught in the synagogues or at the
temple, where all the Jews come together. I said nothing in
secret. Why question me? Ask those who heard me. Surely
they know what I said" (John 18:20-21).

The trial was not going well. Jesus was having no part
of it. Frustrated, "One of the officials nearby struck him in
the face. 'Is that any way to anwer the high priest?' he demanded. 'If I said something wrong,' Jesus replied, 'testify as
to what is wrong. But if I spoke the truth, why did you strike
me?' " (John 18:22-23). Despite their abuse he remained calm.
He was not going to be baited into an angry response.

Only when the truth of his identity was on the line did Jesus respond directly to a question. "The high priest asked him, 'Are you the Christ, the Son of the Blessed One?' 'I am,' said Jesus. 'And you will see the Son of Man sitting at the right hand of the Mighty One and coming on the clouds of heaven'" (Mark 14:61-62). Caiaphas drew himself up in righteous indignation. He "tore his clothes" (Mark 14:63) in the ancient Jewish sign of grief at a serious violation of the Law. " 'Why do we need any more witnesses?' he asked. 'You have heard the blasphemy. What do you think?' They all condemned him as worthy of death" (Mark 14:63-64). The Sanhedrin at this point turned even nastier. "Some began to spit at him; they blindfolded him, struck him with their fists" (Mark 14:65).

Since the Romans had reserved for themselves the right of capital punishment, the Sanhedrin had to present Jesus to the Roman authorities in such a way that they too would judge him guilty of death.

Pontius Pilate   This was not hard to do. The Romans were notoriously quick on the trigger against anyone suspected of subversion. And that was precisely the charge under which the Sanhedrin brought Jesus to the Romans. "We have found this man subverting our nation. He opposes payment of taxes to Caesar and claims to be Christ, a king" (Luke 23:2). The Roman investigation of these charges would be cursory, at best. The Governor of Judea, Pontius Pilate, would conduct it himself.

Pilate had been governor since A.D. 26. A bureaucrat on the make in Rome's foreign service, he had been assigned to the tiny but troublesome territory of Palestine rather than to a more promising post in Egypt or Dalmatia. The Jewish historian Philo reported that Pilate's rule in Judea was marked by "corruption, violence, depradations, ill-treatments, offenses, numerous illegal executions, and incessant, unbearable cruelty."[9] He dismayed pious Jews when he confiscated temple funds to build an aqueduct. He offended their sensitivity to idolatry, by ordering to Jerusalem soldiers carrying banners decorated with images of the emperor.

This man held the power of life and death. But just as

Jesus had refused to bow to the Sanhedrin, he also rejected Pilate's authority. He was not at all impressed with the trappings of Roman rule. Pilate had power—the steel of the Roman legions—but he did not have legitimacy. Pilate, and the Romans he represented, had no right to be in charge of Judea. Their rule was based on conquest, on violence, on fear. Jesus refused to play Pilate's power game. He showed him no special deference. "Pilate said, 'Don't you realize I have power either to free you or to crucify you?' Jesus answered, 'You would have no power over me if it were not given to you from above'" (John 19:10-11), Nor did he try to defend himself. "Pilate asked him, 'Aren't you going to answer? See how many things they are accusing you of.' But Jesus still made no reply" (Mark 15:4).

He was similarly silent when Pilate sent him briefly to Herod Antipas, who was visiting Jerusalem for the Passover. Herod "was greatly pleased, because for a long time he had been wanting to see him" (Luke 23:8). Jesus stood quietly before Herod, seemingly helpless, but armed with the nonviolent strength of his personality. Herod "plied him with many questions" (Luke 23:9). Luke suggests that Herod's intentions may have been frivolous. "From what he had heard about him, he hoped to see him perform some miracle" (Luke 23:8). But Jesus was not about to do tricks to titilate the tetrarch.

The questioning took a more serious tack. "The chief priests and the teachers of the law were standing there, vehemently accusing him" (Luke 23:10). Herod could have declared him guilty of the charges. Although it would have no legal effect—they were in Judea, outside Herod's jurisdiction—his verdict would have been another nail in Jesus' coffin. But something about his silence would not let them drive it in.

Undoubtedly Jesus felt, under the circumstances, that any response would be counterproductive. It would only provoke more heated accusations. His best defense was to let his accusers blow off steam, let their charges be exposed as groundless. He stood on his dignity as one wrongly accused. He would face the ordeal on his own terms. His silence frustrated Herod, but did not provoke him to anything stronger than verbal abuse. "Herod and his soldiers ridiculed and mocked him.

Dressing him in an elegant robe, they sent him back to Pilate" (Luke 23:11). Luke adds one final comment about these partners in crime. "That day Herod and Pilate became friends— before this they had been enemies" (Luke 23:12).

Before the Romans again, Jesus probably realized that, given Pilate's reputation, his fate was sealed. He might have tried to ingratiate himself, picking up on Pilate's attempt to start a metaphysical conversation. "What is truth?" Pilate had asked (John 18:38). He might have pursued the governor's initial reluctance to convict: "I find no basis for a charge against this man" (Luke 23:4). He might have won Pilate over to his side. Since the accusations against him were baseless, he could have explained them away to the governor's satisfaction.

But even if he had been successful, it would have been only a short-term gain. Had he engaged in dialogue and won Pilate's approval, he would have lost it a few minutes later when Pilate succumbed to the pressure of career ambition. "If you let this man go, you are no friend of Caesar. Anyone who claims to be a king opposes Caesar" (John 19:12). That was enough. Whatever meager residue of justice Pilate possessed evaporated in the harsh reality of imperial politics. Threatened with accusations of disloyalty, he pronounced the death sentence.

Ironically, the unfavorable report to Caesar he had tried to avoid by condemning Jesus actually did happen a few years later, in A.D. 35. Pilate had broken up a religious procession of unarmed Samaritans by ordering his troops to attack them. The indignant Samaritans lodged a complaint with Pilate's immediate superior, the governor of Syria, Vitellius. He sent Pilate to Rome to explain his actions to the emperor, Tiberius. That was the end of the line for Pilate. We know nothing about him after that. He dropped out of history.

The Soldiers   During his ordeal before Pilate—it could hardly be called a trial—Jesus already suffered at the hands of Roman soldiers. At one point in the interrogation they had taken him to the basement of the Antonia fortress where they administered a systematic beating on Pilate's orders (John 19:1). These troops were typical of those who secured the Pax

Romana by their brutality. Most Roman soldiers were themselves victims of a particularly brutal discipline. Many had been flogged for trivial reasons. They had seen comrades branded as traitors and even crucified for the minor offense of having been out of range of a trumpet call. The cruelty they experienced was deliberate. It was designed to instill a sullen ferocity that would find its outlet on whomever they were fighting at the time, or on the conquered peoples whose lands they occupied. The sadistic streak which inevitably resulted from the way they themselves had been treated, guaranteed that they would inflict gratuitous pain on Jesus. They would enjoy beating him up. Not only did they flog him with the standard equipment for such occasions, leather straps studded with fragments of bone and metal, but "the soldiers twisted together a crown of thorns and put it on his head. They clothed him in a purple robe and went up to him again and again, saying 'Hail, O king of the Jews.' And they struck him in the face" (John 19:2-3). Jesus suffered the pain and humiliation in silence.

When the death sentence finally came, the Roman execution squad took over. "Finally Pilate handed him over to them to be crucified. So the soldiers took charge of Jesus" (John 19:16). It was nothing personal, they had nothing against him as an individual. Their job was efficient crucifixion. Hurt the prisoner enough to suffer, but not enough to faint. Fasten him to the cross, with spikes if necessary, then hoist him up in a public place where everyone could see the agony, where his torturous death should serve as a deterrent to others. Stay around until he died, to make sure nobody interfered. They didn't have to wait long for Jesus, only a few hours. As a bonus for the job the execution squad got to keep any personal belongings the victim carried. Jesus had only what he was wearing. "They divided up his clothes by casting lots" (Matthew 27:35).

Despite the pain they were causing him, pain he knew would shortly lead to his death, Jesus was able to rise above any resentment he felt for these final enemies. "Father, forgive them, for they do not know what they are doing" (Luke 23:34).

The execution of Jesus, the Galilean teacher who had antagonized some highly placed Jews, had been a minor moment for the Romans. An unexceptional governor had ordered the usual death sentence on someone who had caused a relatively minor nuisance to the Empire. The whole affair was an example of what the philosopher Hannah Arendt has called "the banality of evil."

JESUS' ATTITUDE

When we survey Jesus' response toward all his enemies, we see that it was a mixture of courage and prudence. He often dodged the dangers—passing unharmed through the lynch mob in Nazareth (Luke 4:30); avoiding antagonizing Roman soldiers during his travels; "purposely staying away from Jerusalem because the Jews there were waiting to take his life" (John 7:1); hiding on the Mount of Olives when the heat was on from the Sanhedrin. But when face to face with his enemies he did not flinch. He maintained his dignity and protected his principles. He never compromised with the truth, and always occupied the high moral ground, come what may. When enemies are completely wrong and their actions are utterly evil, Jesus showed that the only morally acceptable behavior is to stand firm, and hope that your courage will nudge them toward changing their ways. Immediate dialogue is impossible.

Jesus always respected the person of his adversaries, even when he disagreed with their position. He never responded with self-defensive counteraggression, never helped spin higher the spiral of enmity. His respect for persons, his holding on to truth in tight situations, spelled out the meaning of his teaching about enemy love.

His earliest followers showed, after his resurrection and ascension, that they had gotten the message. Within a few short weeks after his death, inspired by their experience with their risen Lord, they went about doing the same kinds of things he had done, carrying on his work. As their Master had run into opposition, so did they. He had said, "Do not suppose that I have come to bring peace on the earth. I did not come to bring peace, but a sword" (Matthew 10:34). The sword meant "division," as we know from Luke's version of his words (Luke 12:51). The disciples' healing and preaching brought about the same kind of division Jesus had done—and gave them the opportunity to exercise the same kind of courage and prudence in the face of the enemies they soon had to face.

After healing a crippled beggar, Peter and John were arrested and brought before the Sanhedrin. They spoke boldly: "It is by the name of Jesus Christ of Nazareth, whom you crucified but whom God raised from the dead, that this man stands before you completely healed" (Acts 4:10). The Sanhedrin ordered them "not to speak or teach at all in the name of Jesus" (Acts 4:18). But, instead of obeying, Peter and John replied, "Judge for yourselves whether it is right in God's sight to obey you rather than God. For we cannot help speaking about what we have seen and heard" (Acts 4:19-20). They kept on preaching about Jesus, and they kept on healing. So they were arrested again. And again they stood firm. At this point Peter pronounced their guiding principle, in words that ought to be engraved on the consciences of all peacemakers, "We must obey God rather than men" (Acts 5:29).

Those whose power was shaken by their actions responded in the way of power. They tried to put these preachers and healers out of circulation. The disciples frequently found themselves in prison. They were thrown in jail so often that, as theologian William Stringfellow has suggested, the Acts of the Apostles might more appropriately be entitled the Arrests of the Apostles. But they suffered more than arrests. They were flogged (Acts 5:40). One of the early believers, Stephen, was brutally beaten to death (Acts 7:57-60). At that point a persecution broke out against the church at Jerusalem. Prudently, most of the early Christians left town. "All except the apostles were scattered throughout Judea and Samaria" (Acts 8:1).

Prudence also dictated many of the moves the Apostle Paul made when he faced hostility. He wasn't about to die prematurely, if he could help it. In Damascus, shortly after his conversion, some of his former associates conspired to kill him. "But his followers took him by night and lowered him in a basket through an opening in the wall" (Acts 9:15). Paul often escaped death by discreetly departing the scene. During his first visit to Thessalonia, jealous Jews "rounded up some bad characters from the marketplace, formed a mob and started a riot in the city. They rushed to Jason's house in search of Paul" (Acts 17:5), who, fortunately, wasn't there. "As soon as it was night, the brothers sent Paul away to Berea" (Acts 17:10). After another riot, this time in Ephesus, he again quickly took his leave. "Paul sent for the disciples and, after encouraging them, said good-by and set out for Macedonia" (Acts 20:1).

Paul was arrested for the final time during a riot in Jerusalem. He continued to maneuver adroitly to preserve life and limb. The Roman commander ordered Paul to undergo intensive interrogation to find out the cause of the riot. "He directed that he be flogged and questioned in order to find out why the people were shouting at him like this" (Acts 22:24). Paul knew that, as a Roman citizen, he was legally immune to such treatment. "As they stretched him out to flog him, Paul said to the centurion standing there, 'Is it legal for you to flog a Roman citizen who hasn't even been found guilty?'" (Acts 22:25). No flogging.

The commander sent Paul under heavy protective custody to the Roman governor Felix in Caesarea. This worthy successor of Pontius Pilate kept Paul in prison for two years. "He was hoping that Paul would offer him a bribe, so he sent for him frequently and talked with him" (Acts 14:26). When the next governor, Porcius Festus, seemed on the verge of condemning him, Paul played his Roman citizen card again. This time he demanded a trial before Caesar. Festus said, "You have appealed to Caesar. To Caesar you will go" (Acts 25:12). The Acts of the Apostles ends with Paul under house arrest in Rome for two years awaiting trial.

A TERRIBLE MISREADING

After the Roman empire faded into history and Christianity became the dominant religion of Europe, many of its adherents adopted the ways of Roman power. All too often Christians-turned-Romans treated their Jewish brethren with an extraordinary degree of cruelty. We read sadly of synagogue burnings, forced conversions, isolation into ghettos, beatings, and mob murders.[10] Christians anti-Semitism was often rationalized on the basis of a faulty reading of the Gospels, namely, that Jews are a cursed race because they killed Christ.

The Gospel of John, especially, often states that "the Jews" were enemies of Jesus. "The Jews persecuted him" (John 5:16). "The Jews picked up stones to stone him" (John 10:31). "The Jews led Jesus from Caiaphas to the palace of the Roman governor" (John 18:28). But Jesus himself was Jewish. He was born a Jew, raised a Jew, and died a Jew. From the point of view of a typical Jewish person at the time, Jesus was an impressive rabbi, a teacher learned in the Law and the ways of God. He was another Jewish martyr, killed by the Romans.

In most instances where John uses "the Jews," the other Gospels speak of Pharisees or Scribes or chief priests. We should, it seems, understand John's phrase restrictively, for those relatively few religious authorities who were antagonistic to Jesus. His earliest readers may have understood perfectly well what John meant by "the Jews." But subsequent generations of Christians who had all too often succumbed to the poisonous prejudice of anti-Semitism, read the phrase as an indictment of a whole people.

Those who deplore the death of Jesus at the hands of his enemies must also deplore the deaths of all Jews at the hands of their enemies—who all too tragically often considered themselves spiritual heirs of that same Jesus. Far from representing Jesus' spirit, anti-Semitism reflects the attitude of Jesus' enemies. He identified himself with all the suffering people of history. "Truly I say to you, as you did it to one of the least of these my brethren, you did it to me" (Matthew 25:40).[11]

Anybody who wants to hurt another human being, wants to hurt Jesus, becomes an enemy of Jesus today. Unfortunately, many of his enemies are alive and well in the world right now. Some of them may at times become our enemies as well. We need to examine carefully but urgently the way we can follow Jesus and love them, as he did.

DISCUSSION QUESTIONS

1. In what ways was Jesus a threat to the Roman Empire?
    Would the Roman authorities have gone after him even-
    tually even if he had not been turned over to them?

2. What approach to religion today is the contemporary coun-
    terpart of the Pharisees of Jesus' time? If Jesus were here
    now in the same way as he was in those days, would some
    of these people again be his enemies?

3. The Frankish chief Clovis said that if he had been around
    at the time of Pontius Pilate Jesus would never have been
    crucified. If you had been around at the time of Jesus, how
    would you have been likely to react to his enemies?

4. Do you agree that Jesus' execution was an exercise in the
    "banality of evil"?

5. Who are Jesus' enemies today? In the spirit of Jesus, what
    response ought to be made to them?

CHAPTER FOUR

MAKING SENSE OF ENEMY LOVE

Jesus' formula is precise: "I tell you who hear me: Love your enemies, do good to those who hate you, bless those who curse you, pray for those who mistreat you" (Luke 6:27-28). It expresses in clear, straightforward language the ethical implications of the Peace Myth. The most productive response to enemies is not to try to overcome them, but to build rapport with them: bless them, do good to them, love them. Enmity brings hurt and destruction. Love brings help and healing. Enemy love strikes at the root of hostility. The Latin word for enemy is the negative of *amicus*, friend, which is derived from *amare*, to love. Enmity develops from a lack of love. The radical cure for enmity is to put love there.

72

Jesus did not say "Like your enemies." Liking is an emotional response we can't always conjure up. It's feeling good about somebody. Jesus was more realistic than that. His sense of psychology was sound. If we try to stir up pleasant feelings toward somebody who is bent on doing us harm, we waste a lot of psychic energy. So we don't spend time trying to like people who want to hurt us. Nor should we be disappointed in ourselves when we have unpleasant feelings about them.

Love is deeper than liking. It's a concern for the genuine good of the person. We can love without liking. What the enemy is doing makes us feel sad, or afraid, or bitter. But deep down we want that person to straighten out and get back to a more normal existence. We acknowledge our negative feelings. But we don't let ourselves be dominated by them. We rise above them, and try to look to the humanity of our enemy. That's what Jesus did with the Pharisees, when he suggested they take a more humane approach to the Law. It would help them to loosen up, suffer less from scrupulosity, feel more joy in life. He rose above his resentment of Judas when he called him "Friend." Come back, he meant, we can still get along. He saw the battered condition of the execution squad, and prayed that they be forgiven their cruelty toward him.

Believing in enemy love doesn't mean we naively ignore the conditions of modern urban life. After a day at the 1984 New Orleans World's Fair my wife and I were waiting late at night for a bus back to the apartment where we were staying. The prototypical scowling young man suddenly materialized a dozen feet away from us, apparently intent on taking the same bus. My wife expressed her apprehension. We were out on the street late at night, not many other people were around. I didn't see much danger. I thought the street sufficiently lighted, the traffic sufficiently abundant, and our attitude sufficiently confident. But the next morning we heard on the news that a man my age with his wife had been robbed at knifepoint close to the place and at about the same time we had been waiting for the bus the night before. The victim was in the process of handing over his money when the robber for no apparent reason began stabbing him. He died. After that I was more alert on the streets of New Orleans.

The scowling young man waiting for the bus with us had intended us no harm, had not been our enemy in any sense. We didn't project hostile intentions on to him, but we did realize, my wife more consciously than I that night, that danger lurks in any large city in the United States today. An enemy could confront us at almost any time.

Sometimes the enemy will be so overwhelmingly strong and locked into such a destructive course that it seems suicidal to resist. Police advise mugging victims to give up purse or wallet, even submit to sexual assault rather than fight back. Since we can't love if we're dead—or at least love after death is not what Jesus was talking about—we may have to give in to some enemies temporarily. But submission is not our final response, even if we have to resort to it occasionally. We don't love when we let the enemy wallow triumphantly in ugliness.

ENEMY LOVE IN ACTION

Jesus taught an active response to enemies. Scripture scholar John Piper spelled it out: "First, enemy love is ready and willing to meet the *physical* needs of the enemy. 'If your enemy is hungry, feed him; if he is thirsty, give him drink' (Romans 12:20). Enemy love is disposed to do good to the enemy (I Thessalonians 5:15) and therefore is not content to let him suffer when it has the power to help . . . Second, enemy love desires and seeks the *spiritual* welfare of the enemy. The . . . Christian is to 'bless' him."[1] The "blessing" can take many forms, such as silently absorbing abuse, reaching out to offer emotional support, showing genuine concern for the enemy's distraught state.

One morning in the spring of 1984 an armed and desperate escaped convict walked into the rural Tennessee home of seventy-three-year-old Louise Degrafinried with a shotgun at her husband's back. The woman looked at him quietly, refusing to be intimidated. "You sit down here," she said. "I don't want no violence. I am a Christian lady and I want you to put that gun down." He did. "Lady, I'm hungry, I haven't eaten in three days." She fixed him a breakfast of bacon and eggs. After he finished, she asked him to pray with her. Then she walked outside with him where he surrendered to a highway patrol officer.

Later that same day, a few miles away, another neighbor took a different approach to the same kind of enemy. Two other escaped convicts emerged from the woods into his back yard where the fifty-nine-year-old man was grilling steaks. Knowing the escapees were in the area, he had armed himself with a 45-caliber pistol. When he tried to pull it out to defend against the intruders, one of them shot and killed him. They stole his car, kidnapped his wife, and sped away out of the state.

In loving an enemy we try to follow the direction of the Peace Myth and work toward a rapprochement. We do not concentrate exclusively on our own protection. We look out for the other. We rise above our immediate reaction, which is to draw back, close in. This defensive reaction is so reinforced by social patterns that it seems normal. Many think it's an "instinct" for self-preservation. But it's not. It's a culturally learned response to a threatening presence. Once we know we're not bound by that response, we can decide to take a different course.

As enemies perceive that we care about them as well as about ourselves, we have a chance of diminishing their threat. If they sense we are not about to attack them to protect ourselves, they are less likely to be rigidly defensive. They might even become somewhat open to a possible change in their position. The poet Allen Ginsberg told about a time he was walking in New York's Central Park when a man with a gun jumped out of the bushes demanding money. "Sure, I'll give it to you," Ginsberg said. "But first let's have a cup of coffee. I'd like to talk to you about it." They went across the street into a cafeteria, the assailant a step behind, hand in his coat pocket. Ginsberg listened to the man's story. At the end of the conversation he took out his wallet. But the robber said, "I can't take your money. You're a nice guy." Ginsberg had "blessed" the would-be robber by sharing his burdens. He also got out of a tight squeeze gracefully.

The Soviet Union invaded Czechoslovakia in the summer

of 1968 with a half-million Warsaw Pact troops. Soviet leaders expected to overwhelm the weaker Czech army and have the situation under control in three days. They did not count on the determined resistance of the Czech people, which turned out to be almost completely nonviolent. Czech leaders ordered the army to remain in its barracks, not to engage the invading forces. Soviet tanks were met by a massive outpouring of unarmed people. In city after city they surrounded the tanks and began talking with their crews. Soviet troops were puzzled. They had been told they would face armed opposition. They were ready for battle; they were not prepared for conversation. Soviet soldiers began to develop morale problems. Many had to be withdrawn. Although the invasion was a military success, its real aim—changing the direction of Czech domestic policy—was frustrated by the widespread nonviolent resistance. Eight months later Czech officials negotiated a compromise position. Instead of three days the struggle lasted for eight months, and still did not bring about the results the Soviets had initially desired.

The Czech people had met the enemy nonviolently. While some might argue that their resistance was pragmatic and self-serving, I see it as a realistic example of Jesus' love of enemies. Our human loving is always imperfect, always mixed with a degree of self-interest. The point of the Czech resisters was that they did not harm the invading soldiers, but tried to make them see that everybody's best interest would be served if they turned around and left the country. Not incidentally, the Czechs suffered far fewer casualties and their national life underwent far less trauma than their Hungarian neighbors had gone through a dozen years earlier in a similar encounter.

Enemy love is always directed toward the person of the enemy, not toward the destructive actions the enemy is performing. These we acknowledge straightforwardly for what they are. Enemy love is not simplistic. But it is capable of reversing evil actions precisely because it respects the persons involved in them.

Sara Corson, a United States citizen working in a remote region of Latin America, feared that soldiers in a nearby military camp would set about eliminating the Americans in their zone. When soldiers crashed into the village and surrounded her house one night, she was ready for them. She would try to meet their violence with her love. She tells what happened:

> I found myself stepping up to the closest soldier and speaking words I could never have thought to say. "Welcome, brother," I called out. "Come in. You do not need guns to visit us." . . . I raised my voice and repeated, "You're all welcome. Everyone is welcome in our home."
>
> At that the commander ran up to me, shoved the muzzle of his rifle against my stomach, and pushed me through the door into the house. Thirty soldiers rushed into the house and began pulling everything off the shelves and out of drawers, looking for guns . . .
>
> "What are you Americans doing down here . . .?"
>
> "We are teaching self-help projects to the hungry and we are teaching the Bible."
>
> "That tells me nothing," he responded. "I have never read the Bible in my life. Maybe it is a communist book for all I know."
>
> I picked up a Spanish Bible and turned to the Sermon on the Mount. "We teach about Jesus Christ," I said, "God's son who came into this world to save us. He also taught us a better way than fighting. He taught us the way to love. Because of him I can tell you that even though you kill me, I will die loving you because God loves you. To follow him, I have to love you too."
>
> "I don't believe it."
>
> "You can prove it, sir. I know you came here to kill us. So just kill me slowly, if you want to prove it. Cut me to pieces little by little, and you will see you cannot make me hate you. I will die praying for you because God loves you, and we love you too."
>
> The soldier lowered his gun and stepped back. Clearing his throat, he said, "You almost convince me you are innocent—but I have orders to take everyone in the house . . ."

They marched us two by two at gunpoint down a trail
to where a truck was waiting on the one little road that
came into our village . . .

Suddenly the soldier changed his mind: "Halt!" he com-
manded. "Take only the men. The women will come with
me."

He led us back to our home, saying, "I don't know why
I am doing this. I was about to take you into a jungle
camp of over a thousand soldiers. I know what they do
to women prisoners. You would be abused many times.
I cannot take you.

"In our army no one breaks an order," he continued
sternly. "I have never broken an order before, but for
the first time tonight I am refusing to obey an order. If
my superior officer finds out that you were in this house
when I raided it, and that I did not take you, I will pay
for it with my life." He strode to the door, stopped, and
looked back again.

"I could have fought any amount of guns you might
have had," he said, "but there is something here I cannot
understand. I cannot fight it."[2]

The enemy love Jesus advocated means persevering
through difficult, even painful experiences. It means not being
intimidated by hostility, but resolutely trying to understand
what's behind it. It means trying to reach the persons expressing the hostility, engaging them in the human interaction
necessary to defuse it. Enemy love at its best is nonviolent.

Loving any enemy nonviolently means first of all to put
aside notions of winning. Rather than defeating them we want
a mutually acceptable solution to our quarrel. In the language
of games theory it's called a win-win outcome. Both sides
achieve some of their objectives and are satisfied with the
overall results. Seeking a win-win result means accepting the
partially good intentions of the enemy and working with them.
We realize that the results we struggle for will not conform
entirely to our preferred blueprint, but we hope that the mixture of both sides' assets will endow the end product with a
richness that our way alone could not give.

UNDERSTANDING

A nonviolent approach to any enemy involves three phases: understanding, focusing, and negotiating.

The most basic step is to figure out what's really happening. We have to know the enemy. No matter how different their customs, language, ways of acting, we keep reminding ourselves that they are human beings—caught up in a process we don't like, but basically flesh and blood as we are. People are notoriously unpredictable, often difficult. If I myself am sometimes angry, depressed, frustrated and fearful, I can understand how my enemies are, too. If I look at the world from my own perspective, accepting my interpretation as reality, my enemies probably do the same. They may not hear what I say in the way I mean it. They may read motives in me which I don't have. But precisely because my enemies are people, these problems can be worked out. It's difficult. But difficulty is not the same as impossibility. We start with a fundamental respect for our enemies as persons.

As we try to understand what's going on with our enemy, it helps us to be aware of what psychologists call the three stages of social perception. We all start out taking our own frame of reference as universal. We assume that others have it also, then judge their behavior on that basis. When an enemy's actions go counter to what we believe is right conduct, we judge the enemy to be treacherous or criminal or just plain bad. The Christian crusaders followed a religion they considered the true faith. The Moslems they were fighting had to be evil infidels, then, because they obstinately acted contrary to the true faith. Medieval Moslems, for their part, believed that God wanted everyone to live according to the Koran. They had a mission to communicate God's will to all those living in the world of darkness.

Psychologist Carl Rogers outlined the pattern that develops when both sides approach a conflict locked into this first stage of social perception: "One group feels, 'It is perfectly clear that we are right and you are wrong. We are good and you are bad. Consequently, the only possible solution to the problem is our solution, Z.' But the other group has identical feelings. 'We are right and you are wrong. We are good and you are bad. Consequently, the only satisfactory solution to the problem is our solution, Y.' "³ If we stay in this stage, we want to overcome the other side. We harden our hostility.

In the second stage of social perception we put ourselves in the enemies' place, try to see the world as they see it. We find out how their own history and culture have propelled them toward the behavior of which we disapprove. In this phase we are more tolerant about differing points of view. But we continue firm in our own beliefs. We feel confident about the basic rightness of our own position. We may be more tolerant and slower on the trigger, but we're still hoping for a win if it comes to a showdown.

The Sandinista regime in Nicaragua mobilized a large militia, imported helicopters and armored vehicles from Soviet-bloc countries. Its fighting forces were for a while more numerous than any of its Central American neighbors. The Nicaraguan government claimed the move was purely defensive. Guerrillas were crossing their borders from Honduras to the north and Costa Rica to the south. Their chief of state told the United Nations he feared a large U.S.-backed invasion. Maybe he did. I see how it could look like that from his point of view. But in the second stage of social perception we still hold to our own assumption that Nicaragua is a Marxist threat in the region, and feel it is acting improperly in expanding its military forces. These might have been mobilized because of defensive needs, but they might also be an aggressive prelude to an effort to dominate Central America by force. Maybe the U.S. should invade, to eliminate the danger.

In the third stage of social perception we see the relativity of our own viewpoint as well as the other side's. Both are influenced by the experiences we've gone through. Our notions of right and wrong have strong roots in the values of our particular cultures. We may have absolutized these cultural patterns, believed they came from some cosmic order and are valid for the whole human race. In the third stage we examine critically the position of our side as well as the enemy's. We take conscious note of the tendency to project undesirable characteristics on both sides. When accusations are made we first ask whether these are reflections of a need to feel self-righteous, or whether they are accurate to the reality of the situation.

I look again at the history of U.S. intervention in Central America, and I see how much of my country's presence there has served to assure our economic dominance. I watch with distress how a revolutionary government is pushed into the Soviet orbit because of our unwillingness to enter into constructive arrangements with it. I hear Washington officials say that Nicaragua has aggressive designs on its neighbors because it has far more weapons than are necessary for self-defense. I know that the United States, the most heavily armed nation in the world, also has far more weapons than are necessary for our defense. So I strongly suspect that those Washington officials are projecting on Nicaragua's leaders aggressive intentions they are unwilling to admit in themselves.

In October 1983, a terrorist bombing attack killed some 250 American Marines in Lebanon. President Reagan reacted: "We must be more determined than ever that they cannot take over that vital and strategic area of the earth or, for that matter, any other part of the earth." At the time he didn't know who "they" were who were responsible for the bombing, but he projected onto them the desire to "take over" that part of the world. In the third stage of social perception we can understand better both the fear that drove some Lebanese into anti-American actions, and also the American desire to police so much of the globe.

FOCUSING

We continue to try to know the enemy. At the same time we have a better chance of resolving the conflict if we concentrate our energies on the present problem, not past offenses. We keep our attention on specific issues that divide us now, rather than roaming over the broad background of our hostility. If we insist on referring to the larger picture, the solution to the immediate quarrel becomes more difficult. Family feuds can never be resolved if both sides constantly harp on childhood abuses.

U.S. and Soviet negotiators can place the issue of arms

reduction in the context of Soviet expansionism or American neo-imperialism. When they do, they guarantee that they will make no progress toward a treaty. To get results they have to focus the conflict on the precise issue at hand, the numbers and capabilities of each side's weapons. Harvard negotiations professor Roger Fisher calls it "fractionating" the conflict. "By rational extension, almost everything can be related to anything else. The question for each party is whether it would prefer to deal with issues separately or together . . . For example, countries can agree on cooperative development of weather satellites as a separate issue or insist that the subject is intimately connected with military satellites and that a single agreement must cover both aspects of the problem."[4] By concentrating on a single issue at a time, the parties build confidence in the process, confidence that paves the way for broader solutions.

Martin Luther King, Jr. used the spiritual category of forgiveness to illustrate focusing. "Forgiveness does not mean," he wrote, "putting a false label on an evil act. It means, rather, that the evil act no longer remains as a barrier to the relationship."[5] When we forgive we resolve that no matter what happened in the past, that need not be an obstacle to our settling the present problem. Forgiving, or focusing, is essentially future oriented. We concentrate on the present difficulty, looking for a way to work it out from this moment on. Whatever happened in the past—the harsh words, the aggressive actions, the actual damage the enemy did—we decide we will not allow that to stop us from working out our problems now.

Forgiving is not the same as forgetting. We don't close our eyes to what has been done. We don't pretend that all is sweetness and light, that the enemy did not want to hurt us. We forget at the peril of allowing what happened in the past to develop again. We have to keep the overall picture in mind, but our attention is focused on solving the problem now.

NEGOTIATING

The third phase of the nonviolent process involves a back-and-forth communication with the enemy to hammer out a solution we can both live with.

It can start quickly, as soon as we meet the enemy. Or it may take a long time to get going, depending on the enemy's readiness to negotiate. If the other side initially refuses to join in dialogue, we have many avenues of persuasion available, a whole array of nonviolent techniques for bringing about negotiations. The great marches and demonstrations of the civil rights movement were designed to urge the other side to the bargaining table. "Nonviolent direct action seeks to create such a crisis and foster such a tension that a community which has consistenttly refused to negotiate is forced to confront the issue," wrote Martin Luther King, Jr.[6] He called the tension creative.

Those who say that the other side only respects strength usually have physical force in mind. But inner power, spiritual energy, character wholeness, are more effective than physical strength in negotiating with enemies. Realistically, a demonstration of some kind of strength is necessary for effective negotiations. As peace researcher Gene Sharp has observed, "Behind every case of negotiations is the stated or silent—but mutually understood—role of the relative power positions of the negotiators . . . Gandhi said, for example: "I do not believe in making appeals when there is no force behind them, whether moral or material."[7]

Nonviolence relies on moral force. Even the most hardened make concessions to it. In 1943, at the peak of World War II, the Nazis rounded up most of the Jews left in Berlin. One category, Jewish men whose wives were not Jewish, were congregated in a particular prison. In a spontaneous demonstration of courage the wives of these men, hundreds of them, gathered at the prison gates demanding their husbands' release. The Gestapo machine guns on nearby roofs could easily have fired into the crowd. The women, in increasing numbers, presented a strong, unified front in the face of what seemed like overwhelming physical force. If ever a nonviolent action should not have worked, this was it. But the opposite occurred. The Gestapo commanders did not know how to deal with the kind of power they were facing. As the Latin American officer had said to Sara Corson, "There is something here I cannot understand." By the end of the afternoon they had met with the women. The negotiations were simple. The officers spoke reassuringly, and eventually released the prisoners—in the heart of the Nazi capital in the climate of the Final Solution.[8]

In addition to strength, all negotiations call for a degree of trust. We have to expect that the other side will not take advantage of us but will respond in a constructive way. We have to create that condition by showing early and often that our words and actions are not intended to be harmful. At the beginning of interaction with enemies our guard is up, and so is theirs. We can help make the breakthrough by relaxing our guard somewhat, by reaching out to the opponent in an affirmative rather than threatening way. This is what two young women did when they were accosted in Philadelphia one night by a tall man with a knife who demanded money. They didn't have any. He seemed desperate. "If I don't get some money, someone is going to get hurt." In the few moments of stalemate the women began to understand something: the attacker really didn't like to do this. He was miserable. He was frightened, really more frightened than they were. "Come back with us. I have some money in my apartment." "No! Your husband will be there. Some man will be there." The knife threatened. "There's no one there. Honestly. The apartment is empty. Look, trust us. We'll get you the money." He went with them, but kept the knife ready as the three moved down the street. When they got to the apartment, she produced ten dollars. He apologized, said he only needed five, took it, thanked them, and left.[9]

In entering negotiations the cycle of distrust must be broken—unilaterally, usually. Someone has to take the first step. The Philadelphia women showed a degree of trust toward their assailant. They recognized the pressures on him. They treated him as a human being under stress. He responded with the beginnings of trust in them. It was a small degree, cautious at first, but increasing as he saw they really were going to help him. They assumed their adversary was capable of good will. Their lives depended on their being right. They were.

Successful negotiating involves techniques which can be learned. One of them is to separate the people from the problem. This means first of all trying to relate to the enemy as a person regardless of the issues at stake. Try to establish some kind of rapport, some avenue of communication. Then we concentrate on the issues, not allowing ourselves to be put off by personal characteristics we don't like in the other side. The man with the knife may have looked fierce and had bad breath. His t-shirt may have said, "I love the Devil." No matter. The issue was money, and a threat to kill, not his personal idiosyncrasies. They give some clues to what he's thinking, to which we should be very attentive. In every negotiation it helps to see the situation as the other side sees it. We should appreciate the power of their point of view and the emotional force with which they believe in it.

We've got to shift into the second stage of social perception as quickly as possible. When we do, we may revise some of our own views about the merits of a situation. The Czech people who struck up conversations with Soviet tank crews in 1968 found themselves talking with real men who were bewildered by what was happening, not faceless automatons propelling menacing machinery into their midst. This recognition stopped many a firebomb from being thrown at a tank. When our perception starts to change in this way, Roger Fisher and William Ury point out in their book *Getting to Yes*, it "is not a *cost* of understanding their point of view, it is a *benefit.*"[10]

It's especially important, in negotiating, to give the other side a way out. Never back them into a corner, never insist on ultimatums. They should be given options to respond to, not demands to which they must conform. People react poorly to ultimatums. They generally become defensive and look for a way to strike back.

Above all, we must take care to avoid self-righteousness and the kind of moral pressure that humiliates the other side. We recognize their weaknesses, embarrassment, and fears, as we acknowledge our own. We know, with the poet Longfellow, that "If we could read the secret history of our enemies, we should find in each man's life sorrow and suffering enough to disarm all hostility."

PERSONAL POWER

The process of understanding, focusing and negotiating does not happen in three neatly separable stages. Every interaction with the enemy is part of the negotiation. Throughout the whole process we're always searching for more understanding of motives and interests. From the beginning we keep our efforts focused on resolving the present conflict and building future cooperation. The process can't always be put into practice fully, but it is the blueprint for loving our enemies in a practical way.

Its success depends on the right use of the power that every one of us has. Personal power is the ability to be in control of ourselves, to see ourselves as important. We can give or withhold our cooperation, like the Berlin women outside their husbands' prison. We can reach our adversaries as human beings, and change their minds. We can inspire others and rally them to the cause. Our actions can influence the course of events. We are somebody to be reckoned with.

Everyone can have this power. It's more effective in the long run than weapons. Even the most oppressed, the most physically vulnerable, can have some measure of it. At the very minimum it's the power to refuse to agree to oppression. Peace spirituality writer Sister Mary Lou Kownacki tells of a Chinese officer leading a detachment of troops into a remote village in Tibet. All the Buddhist monks but one had fled before the soldiers arrived. When they burst into the monastery they found the one monk standing calmly in the courtyard. The angry commander pulled out his sword and held it to the throat of the unflinching Buddhist. "Do you know who I am? I am he who can run you through with this sword without batting an eyelash." The monk replied, "And do you know who I am? I am he who can let you run me through with a sword without batting an eyelash." That's personal power.

A basic principle of psychotherapy is that a disturbed person can be helped by contact with a normal, healthy person. The bully backs off when confronted with quiet courage. When I respond to provocation calmly and caringly, others sense my inner strength as supportive rather than dangerous. Personal power can emanate like waves of gentle peace. Playwright Karen Malpede illustrated it in her account of an American Green Beret whose unit had been sent to demolish a village in Vietnam. "A six- or seven-year-old girl-child, whose family had all been killed, reached out her hand to his, touched him and begged for her life." He looked into her eyes, and something stirred deep in his own being. He lowered his gun and walked away. After that, for the rest of his tour of duty, he "shot only to miss."[11]

Personal power begins the moment I decide to assume control of my own life. No matter what others do, I am master of myself. The enemy's military might does not guarantee control over me. I have at my center a core that cannot be touched unless I let it be. Once I realize that I have this power, I look at things differently. I see that all human events—political processes, economic activities—can be affected by it. I can then make fundamental decisions about enemies.

I make my own the words of peace poet Daniel Berrigan: "Peacemakers in principle refuse to play enemy to one who names them enemy." If others point me out as their enemy, I do not respond in kind. Gandhi said that in the dictionary of nonviolence there is no such word as enemy. Instead, I would hope to respond in the way Paul outlined: "When we are cursed, we bless; when we are persecuted, we endure it; when we are slandered, we answer kindly" (I Corinthians 4:12-13).

SELF-LOVE

But I can only respond in Paul's way when I love myself enough to grasp the power that I really have. Self-acceptance, fundamental satisfaction with the way I am, is a prerequisite for effective nonviolent action. Erich Fromm called self-love an art. We can learn it, we can practice it, we can improve it.

Self-love is related to two fundamental aspects of our existence: we are alive, and we are dying. Normally we cherish our life and want to enhance it. We reach out to others in the loving exchange we intuitively feel is enriching. But we're also constantly moving toward death. We can see in the adversities we face a shadow of our own death. We can succumb to it long before it happens by bowing to sickness and sadness, resigning ourselves to repeated defeats. The thought of dying can cause us to dislike ourselves. We can thrash about trying to escape the little deaths we know are forerunners of the real thing. We might lash out in frustration, taking it out on others. Charny notes, "We know that people also hate a lot those whom they love the most: Parents hate their children, spouses hate one another, children hate their parents, friends hate one another, colleagues who otherwise respect one another are drawn into complex hate relationships . . . Although our over-riding wish in all of life is to love and be loved, nature has ordained that the pursuit and conquest of love is tied inseparably to accompanying experiences of protest, pushing off, and hatred."[12] The energy that is our life pulsates constantly in the shadow of our death.

But we can come to grips effectively with these two fundamental realities. We can strike a balance between life and death, between love and hate. We can hold on, but not too hard. We can accept ourselves as we are, mortal, not as we would like to be, immortal. We want to improve, to overcome disagreeable traits, but we can have a fundamental acceptance of the finite, terminal person we are.

For that we absolutely need others. The ability to accept ourselves comes from being affirmed by, in Fromm's words, "the simple presence of a mature, loving person."[13] We can love ourselves when and because we are loved by others. If we're lucky, important initial loving came from our parents before we had anything to do with it. They put us on the right track. But whether or not we had that early parental love, we can always do something about it now. Love of others and love of self is a reciprocal process. We reach out to others and, more often than not, find that they respond. We open ourselves to others, and find ourselves becoming more whole. We can't love ourselves by ourselves. It doesn't work. In fact, self-love eludes us precisely when we seek it directly. The trick is to turn our efforts outward. We touch others, and find ourselves being touched helpfully in turn. As Irish Bishop Dermot

O'Mahony has said, "If you go to a place and do not find love, put a little love there, and then you will find love."

Writer Dorothy Samuel tells about a woman carrying an armful of packages overtaken by two young men who came up from behind and moved in on each side of her. Before they could do anything, she smiled at them and told them how glad she was that they had come along. "I was rather nervous on this street—and these packages are so heavy. Would you help me?" Instinctively, they took the packages. The three of them walked along together while the woman cheerfully thanked them and told them how good they were to help.[14] She sensed that encounter held no love initially. She quickly put some there, and then received at least enough to let her go on her way unharmed. We can all react to life the way that lady did to the threat. We can do something about self-love by seeking affirmation from others, especially from people we respect. We put a little love there first, and then, more often than not, the affirmation comes.

This does not mean that self-love is the underlying motivation in our relationships. But it does mean that we recognize the dialectical nature, the back-and-forth character, of the process. Paradoxically, the more we give, the more we receive. "Whoever sows sparingly will also reap sparingly, and whoever sows generously will also reap generously" (II Corinthians 9:6). We sow the love, the genuine caring for others we bring to our relationships. We reap the love of others, which directly improves our own self-love, the foundation of self-confidence, the indispensable ingredient for loving our enemies.

LETTING GO

As we become more self-confident it's easier to conduct the necessary ongoing review of our possessions. Our aim should be to nurture an attitude of letting go, what spiritual writers traditionally called detachment. This ongoing review is necessary if we are to have leeway in negotiating acceptable solutions to conflicts. Adequate self-love, basic satisfaction with what we are, lets us live without feeling we need so many things for our security.

That doesn't mean we have to live in poverty, although it might sometimes be necessary. The purpose of material goods is not to compensate for our insecurity. They can't do this. Only proper self-love can. Material things should rather enhance human dignity. They help us achieve a level of decency. We appreciate Gandhi's wisdom: "If we are to be non-violent, we must then not wish for anything on this earth which the meanest or the lowest of human beings cannot have."[15] Everyone in the world should have the opportunity for a decent life.

Decency is not the same as luxury. If I have much more than I need and others have much less, the imbalance—which is a form of injustice—is a cause of enmity. People who are living a subdecent life have legitimate ground for feeling hostile to me if I have more than what is decent. Gandhi put it this way: "If each retained possession only of what he needed, no one would be in want, and all would live in contentment . . . The rich should take the initiative in dispossession with a view to a universal diffusion of the spirit of contentment. If only they keep their property within moderate limits, the starving will be easily fed, and will learn the lesson of contentment along with the rich."[16]

Dorothy Samuel had friends who returned home after a summer camping trip to find their house had been broken into and thoroughly ransacked. "The first question we all asked was, 'Did they take everything?' The couple exchanged peculiar glances. 'No. They didn't take anything.' 'It gives you an odd feeling,' the wife added dryly, 'to realize there isn't anything in your house even thieves will bother with.' And they exchanged glances again; wry, a little embarrassed, but basically very satisfied. They are not poverty-stricken people . . . They do not live in a slum, nor are they lacking any of the really basic amenities of modern life. They have central heating, plumbing, refrigeration—even a TV, but an old and unattractive set passed down from relatives."[17]

The less we hang onto, the less we fear those persons who would take things away from us. And, reciprocally, the less we fear others for any reason, the less need we have to search for security in things. Even if we don't have great wealth, if we only want it and work toward it, we increase the possibilities for enmity, because we increase our chances of conflict with others who are similarly motivated. Limiting our possessions to the level of decency includes limiting our desire for more. If we put the desire aside we move toward the freedom necessary to negotiate win-win outcomes with any enemy.

The process spirals higher. The more confident we feel, the less we fear others. The less we fear them, the stronger we feel within ourselves. Our sense of personal power grows apace, and with it our ability to deal nonviolently with our enemies, indeed with all the difficult people we run across in our day-to-day living. We can prepare ourselves for unpleasant encounters. We are alert to techniques such as the exercise in empathy described by the Buddhist monk Nhat Hanh, to help us relate positively to people we dislike: "Sitting quietly, breathe and smile and then half-smile. Picture the person who has caused you the most suffering. Examine what makes this person happy and what he or she suffers in daily life. Imagine the person's perceptions; try to see what patterns of thought and reason this person follows. Examine hopes, motivations and actions. Continue until you feel compassion rising in your heart like a well filling with fresh water. Practice the exercise many times on the same person."[18] When it works we take a more relaxed approach to people who for whatever reason have turned out to be difficult. Usually they respond with a corresponding softening of their attitude toward us. The New Testament said, "Perfect love drives out fear" (I John 4:18). But even imperfect love diminishes fear. Our imperfect love of our enemies diminishes their fear of us. Then if they relax their hostility even slightly, we've opened the window of opportunity a crack and, if things go well, can move forward the threefold process of understanding, focusing, and negotiating.

THE BIG PICTURE

We readily understand Jesus' formula of enemy love as a personal ideal. It's noble to love those who want to hurt us. But we have a harder time seeing it as a realistic national ideal. Our nation's enemies, most believe, have to be met by force. It's hard to see how mere love could have stopped Hitler. We are leery of the Munich syndrome, taking steps toward peace which involve giving in to the enemy's demands. This kind of appeasement does not stop aggression, but only encourages the bully to take advantage of weakness.

And so, many say, we have to be tough with an international enemy. The War Myth calls for keeping other nations in check by the threat of force. We must match the enemy's strength, otherwise we may be vulnerable to the enemy's wiles. In the language of international politics it's called the balance of power. In the language of the nuclear age it's called deterrence. We are told that the only realistic approach to a nuclear-armed nation is deterrence's appalling dilemma: keep the enemy at bay by threatening a world-wide holocaust in which we ourselves will also be destroyed. Deterrence advocates call this a mature approach, "the agonizing, uncertain, half-blind effort to choose the lesser evils," as writer Bob Hutchinson put it.[19]

We know in our hearts that this line of thought is misguided and misleading. We are not restricted to the options of appeasement or deterrence. The bishops' peace pastoral advocated the positive approach of negotiations. "The conviction that political dialogue and negotiations must be pursued, in spite of obstacles, provides solid guidance for U.S.-Soviet relations."[20] They urge this course precisely because of the drastic dangers inherent in deterrence. "The diplomatic requirement for addressing the U.S.-Soviet relationship is not romantic idealism about Soviet intentions and capabilities but solid realism which recognizes that everyone will lose in a nuclear exchange."[21]

We don't have to debate the ultimate value of the nonviolent approach to our international enemies, we don't have to maintain that it's the only morally honest stance to take. The bishops' peace pastoral outlined two morally acceptable options: a restricted resort to physical force, reluctantly undertaken as a last resort and involving the least amount of damage necessary to repel the enemy's attack. The other is the totally nonviolent way, refusing to bear arms, striving for "loving reconciliation with enemies."[22] Both options, the bishops wrote, are based on a "presumption which binds all Christians: we should do no harm to our neighbors."[23] The second approach, they said, "best reflects the call of Jesus both to love and to justice."[24] We don't have to put all our apples in its basket. The bishops simply said it reflects the call of Jesus best. They didn't say it reflects that call exclusively.

But at a time when even a restrained use of force against a nuclear-armed enemy can quickly escalate to an all-out conflagration, we will do well to explore nonviolent techniques for dealing with international enemies. The realities of the nuclear age force us to examine the nonviolent alternative more closely. Not only does it best reflect the call of Jesus, but it also holds out significant hope of preserving and even improving our world. The nonviolent approach deserves careful attention in our era of global ideologies and earth-shattering weapons, where surrender can lead to slavery and fighting is suicidal.

Most of us aren't involved in dealing directly with international enemies—unless we're young enough to be pressed into military service and sent to fight them. But young or old, our contribution in a democracy is to create a public climate in which elected officials will be responsive to a nonviolent approach to our nation's enemies. We need to spread the realization that understanding, focusing, and negotiating are the way toward creating a genuine peace. In order to champion this course confidently, we have to take a clear, hard look at the other nuclear superpower which, as Enemy, is the reason we have built weapons capable of sealing the fate of the earth.

DISCUSSION QUESTIONS

1. Under what circumstances would you give in to an attacker on the streets? What response would you prefer to give?

2. What do you think was going on in the minds of those Soviet tank crews who engaged in conversation with the nonviolent people of Prague in 1968?

3. Is it really proper to look for a win-win outcome with enemies who are perpetrating a vicious assault or propagating an evil system?

4. Pope John XXIII wrote in his 1963 encyclical *Pacem in Terris*, "True and solid peace does not consist in equality of arms, but in mutual trust alone." How can we trust someone—or some nation—who has a history of wrongdoing and is even now prepared to take advantage of us if we relax our defenses?

5. The United States is the richest country in the history of the human race. Envy prompts many people around the world to dislike us. How much of our possessions should we as individuals or as a nation be prepared to let go in the interests of peace?

CHAPTER FIVE

BUT WHAT ABOUT THE RUSSIANS?

After World War II, "communism" became, for most Americans, the enemy that took the place of Hitler and the Japanese.

The Nazi blitzkrieg of Europe and the surprise attack on Pearl Harbor had given America the ideal enemy—two nations that were strong, aggressive, and hostile. Their leadership seemed fanatical, their military ruthless, their ideology despicable. We could put aside our internal problems of economic depression and racial segregation and religious bigotry, and concentrate on defeating Hitler and Tojo. It made Americans feel noble about our cause and our country. It also started the factories humming again and created jobs for millions.

At the war's end we faced an enemy vacuum. Bringing the boys home was fine. But the country found itself in a position of world leadership, in contrast to the messy conditions in which almost everybody else was living in 1945. The War Myth had never been stronger in our history. We had faced a global threat to peace and security, and had ground it into the dust. We were unquestionably right. We had defeated the forces of darkness, and stood ready to meet any other international challenges that might arise. New York Times writer Hanson W. Baldwin expressed the mood of the period: "The United States is the key to the destiny of tomorrow. We alone may be able to avert the decline of Western Civilization."[1]

We were driven by a belief, which did not seem naive at the time, in the inherent goodness of American democracy and our free enterprise system. Most Americans believed it was right and just that these blessings be extended to people all over the globe.

THE COMMUNIST MONOLITH

It was easier to avoid a sober self-examination, easier also to avoid deciphering the complexities of the post-colonial era, if we had an Enemy out there to fasten on, to blame for troubles. International communism easily filled the bill. It was authoritarian, not democratic. It espoused socialism, not capitalism. It inspired independence movements in what came to be called the Third World, movements that ran counter to the interests of our wartime friends France and Great Britain. And it claimed aspirations for world supremacy. As the Senate Intelligence Committee later described our view in those times, "The power of fascism was in ruin, but the power of communism was mobilized . . . Coordinated communist political unrest in western countries, combined with external pressures from the Soviet Union, confirmed the fears of many that America faced an expansionist communist monolith."[2]

The monolith, as many saw it, consisted not only of the Soviet military machine, which remained mobilized after crushing Hitler, but also communist party members and sympathizers in western Europe, Asia, Africa, and Latin America. These disparate elements were lumped together in the vision of a worldwide movement that threatened to destroy the United States and everything else that stood in the way of its domination. Since it opposed us and we were in the right, communism must be very, very wrong.

In the decades following the war communism became a useful internal enemy as well. It functioned as a scapegoat for much that was upsetting to American life. The Labor Movement was suspect because of communist infiltration into unions. Civil rights activity was called communist-inspired. The FBI ransacked Martin Luther King, Jr.'s life for evidence of communist links. The peace movement during the Vietnam years was accused of being orchestrated from communist headquarters in Moscow and Hanoi. Communists were alleged to be behind advocates of gun control, moves to abolish prayer in public schools, and busing for racial integration. University professors suspected of secular humanism were said to be laying the groundwork for a communist take-over. Ministers and priests involved in social causes seemed evidence of communist influence in the churches. Advocates of a freeze on nuclear weapons were called communist dupes as late as the 1980s.

Back in the 1940s and 1950s most Americans' understanding of world affairs was fairly elemental. Whatever validity there might have been for seeing an enemy monolith then, events of the 1960s and 1970s should have shattered it once and for all. China's definitive split with the Soviet Union came in 1963. The Soviet invasion of Hungary in 1956, and especially Czechoslovakia in 1968, alienated many western European communists. Armed forces of Vietnam and China fought each other in the late 1970s.

That some Americans persist in portraying world communism as the enemy says more about their personal needs than about international politics. When we read in a 1982 John Birch Society Bulletin that "It is high time we remember that it is Communism, not the U.S., which relentlessly seeks to conquer the world. . . .' In the past decade, Communist power has conquered Laos, Cambodia, and South Vietnam; it has forcibly invaded Afghanistan; it has used Cuban troops to solidify Communist control of Angola and Ethiopia; and it has crushed the aspirations of the Polish people for even a fraction of freedom in their occupied country,"[3] we understand it as evidence of projection, not description of reality. And when William F. Buckley writes that the "business of stopping communist imperialism" is "the moral architecture of the Western alliance," we know that he is thinking in the style of the 1950s more than the 1980s.[4]

China is the largest communist nation in the world. President Nixon, by visiting there in 1972, and President Carter, by normalizing relations in 1979, undermined for good the belief that communism as such is the enemy against whom we are on our national guard. Communism is an ideology that must be faced if we are to understand its power and counteract its appeal. But the object of our arms buildup and military deployment is not an ideology. It is instead a nation, a definitive political entity that happens to proclaim communism as its national spirit. What we really oppose is not communism but the Soviet Union, our superpower rival for world influence.

THE SOVIET ENEMY

The Soviet Union is an international Stranger, the object of our fear and a target for our projection. President Harry Truman wrote in his memoirs that he came away from his first meeting with Stalin, at Potsdam in 1945, convinced that "The Russians were planning world conquest."[5] That theme, "They want to take over the world," was repeated endlessly, until it became an axiom of American life. The Soviet Union was portrayed as poised to extend its power, eager to gobble up weak countries everywhere, held in check only by the military might of the United States.

And yet the postwar history of the Soviet Union does not support the accusation of world conquest. Nor do the statements of its leaders, who insist—as do all world leaders in the 1980s—that Soviet posture is strictly defensive. "Soviet foreign policy," said Foreign Minister Andrei Gromyko in 1983, "is a policy aimed at easing tensions and defusing the tense international system."[6]

It is difficult to know the real intentions of Soviet leaders. British Prime Minister Winston Churchill once described the Soviet Union as "a riddle wrapped up in a mystery inside an enigma." When James Schlesinger was Director of the CIA, he wrote that "the intelligence community can at best . . . construct plausible hypotheses [about Soviet intentions] on the basis of what continues to be partial and often conflicting evidence."[7] Soviet leaders do not communicate well with each other, much less with their own people. Their carefully controlled press prints only what they want people to read, not necessarily what they're really thinking. We outsiders can not know with any confidence what their long-range goals are.

It's conceivable that their intentions are as benign as their statements say. It's also quite possible that their intentions are considerably more sinister. But we don't know for sure. We can't know. We can only guess. We can suspect, and we can assume. The arms race has been propelled, in George Kennan's words, "not by any reason to believe that the other side *would*, but by an hypnotic fascination with the fact that it *could* . . . We stand like two men who find themselves confronting each other with guns in their hands, neither with any real reason to believe that the other side has murderous intentions toward him, but both hypnotized by the uncertainty and the unreasoning fear of the fact that the other side is armed."[8]

Soviet arms could be the result primarily of the same internal pressures we recognize in our own country, including economic benefits, technological advances, and inter-service rivalries. To attribute them to a desire to take over the world is to draw a conclusion unwarranted by available evidence. But people still do it, even those with international experience who should know better. The War Myth is powerful. Projecting aggressive designs on others that one fails to acknowledge in oneself is common. In its 1976 founding statement the Committee on the Present Danger charged, "The principal threat to our nation, to world peace, and to the cause of human freedom is the Soviet drive for dominance based upon an unparalleled military buildup . . . For more than a decade, the Soviet Union has been enlarging and improving both its strategic and its conventional military forces far more rapidly than the United States and its allies. Soviet military power and its rate of growth cannot be explained or justified by considerations of self-defense."[9]

None of the Committee on the Present Danger or other government official knows what Soviet leaders think they need for adequate defense. Yet the accusations continue: they have a lot of weapons, so they must be aggressive. Undersecretary of State Lawrence Eagleburger said it in 1984: "When the Reagan Administration took office, the Soviet Union was engaged in a sustained and impressive military buildup far surpassing any legitimate defensive needs. Moscow seemed bent on going beyond overall parity with the U.S. forces to acquire a measure of superiority."[10] He did say "seemed," a gesture in the direction of uncertainty. We know what weapons the Soviets have, but we don't know for sure why they have them.

If even the CIA is unable to discern Soviet intentions, we have to read worst-case assertions as reflecting the mind of the asserter, not the facts of the assertion. Attributing malicious intentions to Soviet leaders is a sure sign of enemy thinking. We sympathize with people whose inner needs demand an external enemy, whose personal past impels them to imagine evil motives in others, or whose economic interests dictate a constant harping on the Soviet threat. But their approach shouldn't dominate our nation's actions. It's far too dangerous.

In this chapter we are searching for the correct way to apply Jesus' enemy love to the Soviet Union. The hostility between our two nations is deep and long-standing. It fuels the arms race and has pushed the world to the brink of nuclear cataclysm. If we want to reverse that race we need to make an effort to understand our enemy, to see how the Soviet Union looks in light of the Peace Myth.

Right away we run into obstacles. To many Americans there's something spooky about investigating the Soviet Union. We've heard so often that it's an evil empire, an aggressive nation, that it can't be trusted. The Soviet shadow hovers over displays of patriotism from cheering our Olympic athletes to

marching in Veterans Day parades, from flags on the Fourth
of July to linking God and country in our churches. Our
country has to be strong, so their country won't prevail.

Looking squarely at the Soviet Union to figure out what
is threatening about it is analogous to the first time a devout
religious believer investigates the devil. That unique symbol
and source of evil seems dangerous, but it's also fascinating.
I feel a tingle. Maybe I shouldn't be doing this. It's like play-
ing with fire. Maybe I'll get dragged into the evil and be
contaminated by it. Then something pushes me ahead. No,
I have to know more about this adversary, if only to counter
it more effectively.

Investigating the devil turns up as much information
about believers' fears and fantasies as about the power of evil
itself. In the same way, investigating the Soviet Union reveals
as much about American needs and misperceptions as it does
about Soviet policies and intentions. So we begin the investigation, not expecting to find our international devil, but hoping
to be enlightened about our international peril.

OUR PERSPECTIVE

A great deal of information is available about the Soviet Union.
Public libraries contain abundant descriptions of its geography
and culture, extensive studies of its history and foreign policy.
But we should be alert to the perspective with which the facts
are presented. Clarity and truth about the Soviet Union do
not come easily. A visit, a hands-on experience, is helpful but
not conclusive. Some travelers return with nothing but horror
stories about harassments and shortages and police surveil-
lances. What one sees is filtered through one's own interpretive
screen.

History is never written with complete objectivity. The
presuppositions of the writer need to be taken into consideration in evaluating the truth of a particular assertion. In a subject as critical as the nature of the Soviet Union, we have to
be alert to the attitude behind any presentation. Some of what
is written projects the facts in a bad light, dwells on ugly,

unpleasant incidents. It's easy to see enemy thinking in such exaggerated descriptions as this from a 1953 book *Red Rat Race:* "Russia is the most benighted, bedeviled and bedamned country in the world. It has the most oppressed, suppressed and repressed populace, the fewest sports spectacles and diversions, the horsiest women and rottenest liquor, the most brutal rulers and the least personal liberty of any mass of people on earth."[11] The description is so distorted that it seems tongue-in-cheek. But it wasn't. In the 1980s we see it more as a relic of a bygone age than as a helpful beginning to our investigation.

When President Reagan characterized the Soviet Union as an "evil empire," and its leaders as "arch criminals" and "madmen," we recognize the enemy language he was using. We should not automatically dismiss his allegations. We would be better served if we neutralize the biases they reflect and mine the nuggets of truth that may be buried within. While we reject the dehumanization his words implied, we are interested both in what the Soviet Union has done to arouse such antagonism, and why an American official would resort to such strong terminology.

The picture on the following pages has been influenced by the basic conviction in understanding all enemies: that the Soviet Union is a nation of real people—interesting, sometimes colorful, always struggling. We start off well aware that it is not a model of misunderstood innocence. It's not exclusively a peace-loving society driven to extraordinary lengths of self-sacrifice in the face of surrounding hostility. Too much brutality mars its past for any such whitewashing.

On the other hand it's not an evil empire, on a par with the legendary Mongols of Genghis Khan, the historical Nazis of Adolph Hitler, or the mythical Death Star of Darth Vadar. We prospect for the truth somewhere in between the two extreme views. The Soviet Union is essentially like every other nation in being a collection of people bound together by a particular political structure and influenced by a national spirit that combines survival instincts, idealism, and ambition. Its citizens have the same "joys, hopes, griefs and anxieties," in the words of Vatican II, as we all do.

THE LAND AND ITS PEOPLE

In 1980 I visited the Soviet Union for the first time as part of a Pax Christi delegation to meet with representatives of the Russian Orthodox Church. At the end of my stay I remarked to a new friend, "Your country is difficult to understand." "That's all right," she replied, "we don't understand it either."

But Robert Kaiser, former Moscow correspondent for the *Washington Post*, has noted that "The Soviet Union is rich, varied and complex, but in the end not incomprehensible."[12] We can know much about it quickly. Its size, for example: it is the largest country in the world, with over eight and a half million square miles, spanning eleven time zones. The United States, with three and a half million square miles, is less than half as big, and ranks fourth in size, after Canada and China.

Only the population giants India and China surpass the Soviet Union in numbers of citizens. Its 270 million people live in fifteen semi-autonomous republics and speak over 125 different languages. Of the fifteen republics the largest by far is the traditional Russia, containing half the population and comprising three-fourths of the total territory of the Soviet Union. Because of Russia's historical dominance over the other areas that make up the present nation, its name is often applied by outsiders to the entire U.S.S.R.

Soviet people display a vast ethnic diversity. Some are Europeans, in the Baltic republics of Latvia, Lithuania and Estonia, or in Moldavia on the Rumanian border. Others are stalwart sons and daughters of Mother Russia, the land that long inspired poets and artists and beckoned Stalin's daughter to return after fourteen years in the West. Millions more are every bit as Moslem as their Middle Eastern neighbors in Iran and Afghanistan. Still others, Mongols in the east, are thoroughly Asiatic.

Whether contributing to the urban economy or farming in the vast countryside, Soviet people concentrate as people everywhere on the demands of daily living—going to work in the morning, supplying the family's food and clothing, pursuing a career, marrying, taking care of grandparents, finessing the bureaucracy. Most Americans are aware that the Soviet standard of living is lower than in Western Europe or the United States, but—importantly, in Soviet eyes—considerably higher than it was in Russia under the czars. Most Americans know, too, that political freedom is severely restricted. But most Americans seem not to know the internal dynamics that contribute to the suppression of freedom.

A POLICE STATE

Holding this vast, turbulent internal empire together has been a difficult challenge. Centrifugal forces constantly threaten the breakaway of one or another territory or ethnic group from central control. Traditionally the rulers of the land, from the czars to the present, have been strong and dominating, in response to a long history of invasion from outside and anarchy from inside. Kaiser noted, "Russians have little faith in their own capacity to combat anarchy with self-discipline and restraint. The creation of a true dictatorship is all that preserved the Russian nation in the late Middle Ages, and Russians have been relying on dictators ever since."[13]

This tradition explains much in Soviet behavior. Their fear of foreigners and foreign ideas, and their concern about domestic opposition seem almost paranoid to outsiders familiar with Soviet history. But, as Hungarian writer George Konrad has noted, Soviet leaders are not "crackpots, or men possessed, or ideological fanatics. They are mature, dry, stolid, cautious, mistrustful men . . . They don't want to be forced into a corner or see their country humiliated . . . Their historical experience has been one of being regarded with suspicion, of being encircled and attacked."[14]

And so, internally, the country is a police state. The KGB, the Committee for State Security, is notorious for rounding up dissenters, silencing objectors, confining critics in mental hospitals, tolerating no independent press, and restricting its citizens' freedom of movement. Many of these actions, considered repressive from our point of view, may be motivated by a desire to hold on, a fear that any rocking of the boat may in fact capsize it. This is not to say that they are any less harmful to their victims. But we may deal with them differently if we understand them as pragmatic efforts to hold on to power rather than inevitable consequences of communist belief.

THE OFFICIAL PHILOSOPHY

The formal spirit of the Soviet Union was first articulated by Karl Marx and Friedrich Engels in their celebrated *Manifesto of the Communist Party*, published a century ago (1888) in Germany, long before there was a Soviet Union. "The theory of the Communists may be summed up in a single sentence: Abolition of private property," they wrote.[15] They dreamed of a classless society, where no one would exploit anyone else, where the normal controls of government would not be necessary, and where all would contribute according to their ability and receive according to their needs.

The road to this utopia would be rocky. The *Manifesto* declared: "The Communists disdain to conceal their views and aims. They openly declare that their ends can be attained only by the forcible overthrow of all existing social conditions. Let the ruling classes tremble at a Communist revolution."

Marx and Engels had western Europe in mind when they wrote of a Communist revolution. Marx had earlier thought that the American Civil War heralded such a revolution in the United States. But it was in dim, backward Russia that his vision was actually pursued. The charismatic Vladimir Ilytch Ulyanov, who took the name Lenin, led the successful 1917 Bolshevik uprising under the Communist banner. Now in charge, Lenin quickly moved to the next phase outlined by Marx and Engels. The proletariat—the working class—would, after overthrowing inequitable social structures, "centralize all instruments of production in the hands of the state." Lenin decreed: "All citizens are here transformed into hired employees of the state, which is made up of the armed workers. All citizens become employees of one national state syndicate."[16]

According to Marx's blueprint, state control was the

next step toward becoming the ideal society in which, after all class antagonisms and divisions had been swept away, "the free development of each is the condition for the free development of all," in the ringing phrases of the *Manifesto*. Marx's vision contained a powerful message of equality. It would be achieved first by a forcible overthrow of oppressive institutions, which would release people from exploitation. Then history would move forward in a surging wave toward a truly just society.

After the 1917 revolution the vision caught the imagination of millions of people not only inside Russia but around the world. Its appeal combined the idealism of righting wrongs and extending opportunity to all, with a materialism that placed a high value on the prosperity of property—not private property, but communal goods that enhance the quality of life for all. Institutions tied to the past, including religion, the patriarchal family, and a capitalist economy, would be swept aside as people moved to their true human fulfillment.

Some thought that the communist goal of a classless society, materially abundant and free from exploitation, was similar to the Judaeo-Christian dream of *shalom*—a just and peaceful society, the realization on earth of the Kingdom of Heaven. But they recoiled from the means by which that society was to be achieved: by coercion. They also felt that in rejecting religion because of its association with class exploitation, the communists were destroying the only realistic foundation for human fulfillment.

Other critics were quick to point out that communism relegated the individual person into relative insignificance compared to the inexorable movement of social forces. Ideals of freedom and voluntary cooperation, cherished in the west, were minimized. This was especially so in the stage of state socialism, where the individual could be sacrificed for the good of the whole.

But the gut reaction against the communist revolution came from people who had accumulated some wealth and property, and realized that they would lose it in a truly communist society. These were quick to extol the values of freedom—meaning the freedom to keep what they had—while ignoring the values of justice embodied in the communist dream.

Communism in the Soviet Union has functioned more as a national ideal than a guiding philosophy. It provided a framework for interpreting the past. It gave inspiration for dealing with present problems. Over the years the Soviet Union has fulfilled part of the ideal by eliminating the class of wealthy exploiters, doing away with the worst poverty, and bringing a greater degree of decency into the lives of peasants and workers. It also held out the communist ideal to oppressed peoples around the world. Former premier Nikita Khrushchev said that communism would spread precisely because of this appeal: "Our certainty of the victory of communism is based on the fact that the socialist mode of production possesses decisive advantages over the capitalist mode . . . We believe that all working men in the world, once they have become convinced of the advantages communism brings, will sooner or later take the road to struggle for the construction of socialist society."[17]

But the seventy-year history of the Soviet Union has been dominated more by the demands of *realpolitik* and the exigencies of power than the goals of a humanitarian community. Unfortunately for true believers, communism has not produced the model society Marx envisioned. He had predicted that after an initial period of control to consolidate the gains of the revolution, the state would "wither away." Instead, in the decades since 1917 the Soviet Union became fixed in the phase of state control. The 14-million-member Communist Party effectively regulates the nation's life. The state apparatus shows no signs of withering away. Power is in the hands of a few. The image the Soviet Union presents to the world is a sluggish, fearful, totalitarian giant, with a sputtering socialist economy and a very large army. Many of its people have given up. Others struggle to improve slightly their place in the rigid system. Millions receive strength and comfort from their religious faith.

RELIGION IN RUSSIA

A surprising number of Soviet citizens take advantage of the degree of religious freedom available in the country. Although the U.S.S.R. is officially atheistic and church attendance is discouraged, its new 1977 constitution allows freedom of religion to all citizens. It hasn't always been so. Early communist enthusiasts saw religion as a drug which deadened the pain of poverty. They branded it as a shameless shoring up of the exploiting class of wealthy landowners. All religion, they felt, had to be rooted out of the brave, young communist society.

It didn't work. Despite opposition that ranged from harassment to persecution, millions continued to practice the religion of their ancestors. The 1977 constitution acknowledges the reality of religion's persistence: "Citizens of the U.S.S.R. are guaranteed freedom of conscience: that is, the right to profess or not profess any religion, and to conduct religious worship."[18] An official government agency, the Council for Religious Affairs, oversees the operations of the various religious bodies. Its twofold responsibility is to make sure that no non-religious activity takes place, and that the laws guaranteeing freedom of religion are upheld.

At least fifteen million Moslems live in the Soviet Union, mostly in the Central Asian republics in the south. Baptists, the fastest growing religious body, number some five million. Several hundred thousand Protestants live in Latvia and Estonia, where the Evangelical Lutheran Church has long been associated with national identity in those republics. In 1983, for the first time since the 1917 Revolution, the government allowed Lutherans from all over the Soviet Union to gather in Riga, Latvia's capital, to commemorate the 500th anniversary of Martin Luther's birth.

Most of the nation's three million Roman Catholics live in the third Baltic republic of Lithuania which, before annexation in 1940, was a traditionally Catholic country. Jewish citizens of the U.S.S.R. also number close to three million, and comprise the greatest concentration of Jews in any country outside Israel and the United States. The largest religious body, the Russian Orthodox Church, counts thirty million active members, by conservative estimate, more than twice as many as belong to the Soviet Communist Party.

The only officially tolerated religious activity is worship, including baptisms, marriages, and funerals. No educational or social work is permitted. These activities all take place under the tight control of the government. But the mystery of God's power and God's interaction with the visible world embodied in the scriptures and worship of these diverse religious groups remains for many millions a persistent alternative to the stagnant ideology of communism. The early image of antireligious propaganda and the outright persecution of religious believers still dominates western understanding of the Soviet Union. It has been a persistent thread in the antagonisms most Americans feel toward this Enemy.

U.S. OPPOSITION

Within months of the 1917 seizure of power by the Lenin-led Bolsheviks, detachments of American military forces entered the Soviet Union in Murmansk and Vladivostok. Their mission, in that summer of 1918, was ostensibly to protect the munitions and materiel which the Allies had sent to support the Czar's armies during the First World War. Once there, though, the Americans joined troops from Britain, France, Germany, and Poland in an effort to defeat the new regime. The American 339th regiment, called the Polar Bears, fought Bolsheviks in temperatures under fifty below zero in the snow-covered forests of northern Russia that winter. Winston Churchill, Britain's Minister of War at the time, said that the action was intended "to strangle Bolshevism in its cradle."[19]

That initial invasion, although finally stopped by the newly organized Red Army, supplied grounds for Lenin's assertion that the capitalist world would seek to stifle the first communist state. In later years the Moscow government would use the fear of foreign intervention as justification for the stern measures it took against its own citizens.

Through the 1920s the United States refused to recognize the new Russian government. Its reason was partly economic.

Lenin's program had disavowed international debts incurred by the czars. It had also nationalized foreign properties without compensating their owners. But ideology played a part—the desire for stability and property threatened by the rhetoric of world revolution and contempt for capitalism emanating from Moscow. Many in the West took seriously Lenin's 1919 prophecy that "the existence of the Soviet Republic side by side with imperialist states for a long time is unthinkable. One or the other must triumph in the end. And before that end supervenes, a series of frightful collisions between the Soviet Republic and the bourgeois states will be inevitable."[20]

Even after President Franklin Roosevelt gave formal recognition to the Soviet Union in 1933, knowledgeable Americans continued to be uneasy about the philosophy of communism, and about the atrocious conduct of the Soviet government toward its own citizens.

STALIN'S PURGES

The man who maneuvered himself into the revolutionary government's top position after Lenin died, Josef Djugashvili, had taken the name Stalin, meaning "steel." His daughter Svetlana later characterized him as at times confused and weak after the suicide of his wife in 1933. In his state of near paranoia, he suspected anyone and everyone of undermining his power or usurping his prerogatives. Stalin's desire to protect his position was the driving force behind an extraordinary brutalization of people even remotely suspected of being opposed to him.

In the 1930s the man of steel ordered millions of Soviet citizens sent to prison camps, or executed. His secret police often interrogated these prisoners for days, and weeks, without a break. Torture was common. The interrogators threatened reprisals against family members as a way of coercing cooperation in making confessions which implicated others. During the height of the terror the arrest of one person was generally followed by the detention of that person's associates, friends, and family, so that the purge was an ever-escalating process.

According to historian J. N. Westwood, "the fear of the NKVD's knock on the door in the night led to nervous break-downs and suicides."[21] Slave labor gulags teemed as Stalin effectively crushed real and imagined internal opposition.

The purges diminished as Europe neared the brink of a war in which Stalin sensed his country would be involved.

TERRITORIAL TAKEOVERS

Communists the world over were shocked when Stalin signed a Non-Aggression Pact with Hitler in August of 1939. The agreement freed Hitler from immediate concern about the east, so he could concentrate military pressure on the rest of Europe. It also allowed Stalinist Russia to take over some of the smaller territories on its own border.

The Non-Aggression Pact contained a secret section which divided Poland into German and Russian spheres of influence. After the Germans invaded Poland in September of that year, Soviet armed forces entered from the other side. As a Soviet historian put it, their nation "took under its protection" the life and property of some thirteen million people,"[22] including ten million Ukrainians and Belorussians who had been under Polish rule from territorial shifts stemming from historic antagonism.

Stalin's next move, still under cover of the treaty with Hitler, was to annex the Baltic states of Lithuania, Estonia, and Latvia, which had been part of the Russian Empire of the czars. In the spring of 1940 Stalin fostered the formation of communist-led governments in the three countries, while Soviet troops massed on their borders. The governments then formally requested incorporation in the U.S.S.R. as republics. The troops moved in and the takeover was complete. Hundreds of thousands of citizens were deported to concentration camps, accused of anti-Soviet behavior.

Then came Finland. Military action in 1939-40—in retaliation, the Soviets said, for Finnish artillery fire directed against their territory—resulted in the capture of land which became the Karelo-Finnish Republic of the U.S.S.R. In June of 1940 the Soviets announced that Rumania should give up Bessarabia, formerly part of czarist Russia. With the Rumanian army unable to resist, Bessarabia was annexed and became the Moldavian Union Republic of the U.S.S.R.

The United States, needless to say, took a dim view of these moves.

THE GREAT PATRIOTIC WAR

U.S.-Soviet antagonism simmered on the back burner during World War II when both countries joined as allies in the fight against Germany. Hitler had broken the Non-Aggression Pact and ordered his armies to invade the Soviet Union. Russian people suffered terribly in that ordeal. Twenty million of them were killed. But the Great Patriotic War, so the Soviets still call it, united the country in a way that nothing else had ever done. Stalin suspended his attacks against the religious establishment. He enlisted the aid of the Russian Orthodox Patriarch in rallying the people to resist the invasion. The Patriarch contributed church funds to the war effort. His money outfitted a tank batallion, so that tanks bearing names of church saints went into battle with the Germans.

Stalin met President Truman for the first time at the Potsdam Conference in Berlin in July of 1945. During the conference Truman received word of the successful test explosion of the first atomic bomb in the New Mexico desert. The allied leaders had never communicated about the secret project under way at Los Alamos. After conferring with Churchill about how much to reveal to Stalin, Truman decided that he would let the Soviet leader know, as he said later, only in a "roundabout way." The next day Truman casually mentioned to Stalin that the Americans had perfected a new weapon of unusual destructive force. Stalin offhandly responded that he hoped the Americans would make "good use of it against the Japanese."[23] Stalin may have had his own intelligence reports about the atomic weapons, or he may have found out about them only after the Potsdam meeting. He realized that the American president had concealed this vital information from a wartime ally. Neither side trusted the other very far.

Historians are divided about whether the primary motivation for using the bomb was to bring the war against Japan to a speedy end, or to send an intimidating signal to the Soviet Union. Both motives were certainly present. The Soviet Union focused on the second. From their perspective, as one of their historians noted, "By dropping the [atomic] bomb on the Japanese cities, the U.S. imperialists were trying to frighten the world, especially the Soviet Union. It marked the beginning of the aggressive course steered by the U.S.A. toward the establishment of world domination."[24]

As in all cases of attempted intimidation, the threatened party reacts cautiously and shows initial restraint. But its psychological response is an increased dislike and distrust for the intimidator. The implicit threat in the use of atomic weapons made the Soviet Union more defensive and more hostile toward the United States.

THE COLD WAR

After Germany's surrender the Red Army remained garrisoned in Poland, Hungary, Bulgaria, Albania, and Rumania. Communist governments soon took power in those countries. With Soviet support they suppressed local opposition, and began to reconstruct their war-torn nations on the Soviet model. Postwar distrust between the Soviet Union and its former allies resulted in an indefinite split of Germany. The French, British, and American occupation zones were amalgamated at the end of 1946 into what became the Federal Republic of Germany. The Soviet-occupied eastern zone evolved into the Democratic Republic of Germany. Czechoslovakia was the last eastern Europen country to come under Soviet control, in 1948.

On the other side of the world, half a billion more people entered the Soviet sphere when Mao Zedong's forces were victorious in China in 1949. This extended Soviet domination from central Europe to the Pacific Ocean, and from the North Pole to Southeast Asia.

As they saw it, the Soviets had a reasonable excuse for

acquiring this influence. They had been invaded in the last century by Napoleon and in the twentieth century by Germany. They had suffered terribly at the hands of the West. They wanted to have a buffer zone to thwart any future invasions. And, as they were struggling to rebuild their own country from the devastation of war, they welcomed the spread of socialism to their neighbors in the east. Many hoped this spread would be the wave of the future.

But the United States saw it differently. Ambassador Kennan, in his influential *Foreign Affairs* article of July 1947, gave impetus to the impression of the Soviet Union as relentlessly expansionistic. He said it was driven by a fanatical ideology to filling "every nook and cranny available . . . in the basis of world power" and "stopping only when it meets with some unanswerable force."[25] This was the same George Kennan who said later that we shouldn't jump to conclusions about Soviet intentions. As a younger man, in the press of events, he had done just that. His interpretation facilitated the slide of the Soviet Union into the role of Enemy.

Suspicion of this Enemy proved epidemic. General Lucius Clay, U.S. European commander in 1948, expressed it in a moody message: "I have felt a subtle change in Soviet attitude which I cannot define but which now gives me a feeling that it [war] may come with a dramatic suddenness." His cable provoked what the Senate Intelligence Committee later called the "near hysteria" which gripped official Washington. A flurry of agency estimates could find no evidence that the Soviet Union would start a war. But Clay's cable, the Committee said, "had articulated the degree of suspicion and outright fear of the Soviet Union that was shared by policymakers in 1948."[26]

THE NUCLEAR EQUATION

In that same year, 1948, the United States positioned a fleet of B-29 superfortresses in England. From there, armed with atomic bombs, they could reach the Soviet Union in the event of war. U.S. policymakers, in those postwar years of nuclear monopoly, feared Soviet expansion into Western Europe. They warned that if such action did take place the U.S. would retaliate devastatingly with the atomic weapons it alone possessed. The attacks would be directed primarily against Soviet cities. The U.S. might even initiate atomic war, a 1948 National Security Council policy statement implied, in order to remove "the ever-present threat of . . . Soviet military power."[27]

Twelve Western nations, including the United States and Canada, formed the North Atlantic Treaty Organization in the spring of 1949. The U.S. moved quickly to establish air bases in Turkey, posing a nuclear threat on the southern border of the Soviet Union.

A few months later, in August of 1949, the Soviets exploded their own atomic bomb.

Because the Soviet Union had demonstrated that it also had atomic weapons, the United States refrained from pressing the Korean War to the same kind of definitive ending it had accomplished against Japan a few years earlier. The result instead was a 1953 stalemate that kept Korea divided about as it had been before forces from the north invaded the south three years earlier.

The Los Alamos scientists were still busy. In 1952 the U.S. tested its first hydrogen bomb, utilizing the fusion process which produces the sun's energy. The first hydrogen bomb, exploded near the Pacific island of Eniwetok, was a thousand times more powerful than the bomb that had decimated Hiroshima. The Soviets exploded their first hydrogen weapon in 1955. They were matching U.S. nuclear capability as quickly as they could.

FIGHTING FIRE WITH FIRE

During the 1950s U.S. policymakers revised their estimate of Soviet intentions. No longer did they see the danger as an invasion of western Europe and direct territorial acquisitions. Instead, they thought the Soviets were aiming for the subversion and eventual control of any country weak enough to be

susceptible. The U.S. role on the world stage would be to prevent that expansion.

The Hoover Commission in 1954 outlined what it considered the appropriate U.S. response: "We must learn to
subvert, sabotage and destroy our enemies by more clever,
more sophisticated and more effective methods than those used
against us."[28] We would employ against the Soviet Union,
which the Commission described as "an implacable enemy
whose avowed objective is world domination," the same means
we accused them of using. We would not be constrained by
the norms of morality. "After all," as Senator William Fulbright later recalled, "who ever heard of giving the Devil a
fair shake?"[29] We would fight fire with fire. The following year,
1955, the U.S. government began a program of direct intervention in Soviet domestic and foreign affairs. A National
Security Council directive authorized the CIA to "create and
exploit problems for International Communism . . . develop
underground resistance and facilitate covert and guerrilla
operations."[30]

The arena for clandestine confrontation expanded into
the western hemisphere when Fidel Castro's revolutionary
brigades overthrew Fulgencio Battista's regime in Cuba in 1959.
Castro was not a communist at the time. The American ambassador in Havana, Philip Bonsal, wrote, "There was no
serious evidence of effective Communist influence upon the
new Cuban government."[31] But Americans were dismayed
when so many Cubans who had been associated with Battista
were executed shortly after Castro took power. The U.S. welcomed thousands of middle-class businessmen, bankers, admin-
istrators, doctors, and teachers who were starting to leave the
country. Most had at first been overwhelmingly pro-Castro,
but became disaffected as new economic restrictions were
imposed.

In 1960 Castro's reforms included expropriation of
American businesses on the island, notably several oil re-
fineries. The U.S. retaliated by boycotting Cuban products.
Castro turned to the Soviets for help. Their response was
immediate and substantial. They sent tractors and tanks,
military advisors and civilian technicians. They also bought

Cuban sugar and cigars. They built schools and trained doctors. Secretary of State Dean Rusk echoed the enemy language of the 1950s when he labeled this help "part of the powerful offensive launched by the Sino-Soviet bloc against the Third World."[32]

Despite persistent U.S. efforts to overturn his revolution, from the Bay of Pigs invasion in 1961 through assassination attempts in the 1960s and 1970s, Castro was firmly entrenched in power in the mid-eighties, and thoroughly anti-American in his outlook. His ties with the Soviet Union made it possible for the Cuban economy to continue functioning. As *New York Times* correspondent Herbert Matthews wrote, "The Russians saved [Castro's] Revolution and have contributed vitally to keep it going ever since. All predictions that they could not indefinitely sustain the cost—usually rated by guesswork at $1 million or more a day—or that they would get fed up with Cuban bungling, or that a detente with the United States would make Cuba expendable, have proved wrong."[33] With Cuba, the U.S.S.R. had a firm foothold in the western hemisphere.

The Soviets, too, knew how to fight fire with fire, especially in their own backyard. They crushed uprisings in East Berlin in 1953 and squelched the Poznan riots in Poland in 1956. Red Army tanks moved into Hungary later that year to suppress demonstrations which demanded an end to Soviet occupation. Soviet tanks again rolled into an eastern European country in 1968. This time it was Czechoslovakia, to combat Czech efforts to bring about "socialism with a human face." Although, thanks to the spontaneous Czech nonviolent resistance their efforts were not as successful as they would have liked, to most in the West the Soviet fire-fighting machine seemed formidable.

THE ARMS RACE

During the 1950s the United States had produced hundreds of intercontinental jet bombers capable, with the refueling help of air tankers, of dropping nuclear bombs on every part of the

Soviet Union. At that time the Soviet air force was still using piston engine planes. A few of them could reach parts of the northern United States on a thirteen-hour flight from Siberia— although it would be a suicide mission because they couldn't return home. But U.S. territory for the first time was at risk from Soviet nuclear weapons.

Both sides declared that their nuclear capability was defensive. Nikita Khrushchev described the Soviet intentions: "Now that we had nuclear bombs and the means to deliver them, we had no intention of starting a war. We stood firm on Lenin's position of peaceful coexistence. We only wanted to deter the Americans' threats, their aggressiveness, and their attempts to terrorize us."[34] Vice President Nixon spoke for the United States: "Rather than let the Communists nibble us to death all over the world in little wars, we would rely in the future primarily on our massive, mobile retaliatory power."[35]

The Soviets viewed U.S. superiority, which was undeniable, as aggressive. They particularly resented what they considered humiliating expressions of it, such as the U-2 spy planes. The Soviets could detect them on radar, but since the aircraft operated at 70,000 feet, had no way to shoot them down. As Khrushchev recalled, "We were sick and tired of these unpleasant surprises, sick and tired of being subjected to these indignities. They were making these flights to show up our impotence."[36] The humiliation was compounded when the U-2s flew over on days of special national pride— November 7, the anniversary of the 1917 Revolution, and May 1, the day honoring the nation's workers. Of course these were days on which the Soviets paraded some of their latest weapons, important subjects for the spy planes' cameras.

In 1957 the Soviet Union surprised the world by sending the first artificial satellite into orbit. U.S. military analysts concluded that the Soviets had a rocket of sufficient power to deliver an unstoppable nuclear weapon to the United States. The U.S. had already embarked on its own program of building similarly powerful rockets, and quickly surpassed the Soviets in the numbers it produced. The Soviets attempted to counteract U.S. superiority by placing medium-range missiles in Cuba in 1962. Although Khrushchev said the missiles were there to protect Cuba, the American government perceived them as a direct threat against the United States. The Kennedy administration prevailed on Khrushchev to withdraw in return for a promise not to invade Cuba. As Secretary Rusk later summarized the confrontation, "We were eyeball to eyeball, and the other guy blinked."

Being made to blink in the Cuban Missile Crisis was another humiliation for Soviet leadership. Vowing that never again would they be caught in a position of such inferiority, they embarked on their own ambitious military buildup. They decided to place their greatest strategic reliance on large, land-based missiles. By 1970 the Soviet Union had more missiles than the United States, but fewer hydrogen bombs and less flexibility. They were actually surrounded with nuclear weapons. The U.S. had missile submarines in the Atlantic and Pacific oceans, and bombers in Europe and Asia. Britain and France aimed nuclear missiles from the west. China did the same from the east. But by the early 1970s the Soviets had achieved effective nuclear parity in destructive ability. Both sides had the ability to devastate each other several times over. They were now ready to deal with each other as nuclear equals.

DETENTE ON AND OFF

The first Strategic Arms Limitation Treaty was signed in 1972, when tensions were slightly relaxed. The two sides had already accepted some restrictions on their nuclear postures with the Limited Test Ban treaty in 1963, the Non-Proliferation treaty in 1967, and the Outer Space treaty in 1968. In SALT I they agreed not to develop antimissile systems. They also set ceilings, which were fairly high, on the numbers of missiles each side would build.

Under the SALT I umbrella both countries continued to produce huge quantities of weapons. The Soviet Union expanded its naval forces, increased the size of its army, and deployed large numbers of tanks in Eastern Europe. It continued to help revolutionary movements in the Third World. Much of its military allocations was directed toward China, which became even more troublesome after its rapprochement with the United States. In the late 1970s the Soviets put in place a new generation of medium-range missiles, the SS-20, capable of reaching all points in Europe and Asia from bases inside the Soviet Union. These were intended to replace the older SS-4s and SS-5s, which for two decades had been the Soviets' answer to NATO planes and submarines.

The Soviet record of adhering carefully to all its arms control treaties with the United States helped produce a second Strategic Arms Limitation Treaty, signed by President Carter and Brezhnev in 1979. But SALT II was not ratified by the U.S. Senate as detente fell by the wayside at the end of the 1970s. Two events had significant bearing on its demise. The first was the NATO decision in late 1979 to allow the United States to deploy 572 new nuclear missiles in Europe. These Pershing-2 and Cruise missiles, capable of reaching the Soviet heartland, would be under sole U.S. control. The Soviets saw this as a significant escalation of the U.S. threat.

The second event that buried detente was the Soviet action in Afghanistan. Shortly after the NATO decision to accept the new U.S. missiles, the Soviet Union launched a massive military intervention against its small, weak southern neighbor to quell an internal revolt. In December of 1979 almost 100,000 Soviet troops entered that mountainous, nomadic country—and promptly got bogged down in their own Vietnam.

Under the Reagan administration in the early 1980s the spirit of American foreign policy became "prevailing with pride." The U.S. moved boldly ahead in building first-strike weapons like the Trident submarine and the M-X missile. U.S. planners talked openly about winning a nuclear war—even though winning as they described it was a bleak prospect: less Americans than Soviets would be killed, less of America than the Soviet Union would be destroyed, and the U.S. could rebuild its society while the Soviets could not.

The Soviets perceived the United States moving precipitously closer to the brink of a worldwide conflagration. They responded with harsh words and military countermeasures. President Yuri Andropov promised to retaliate for the new NATO missiles by installing short-range nuclear weapons close to the United States. A Soviet fighter shot down a Korean jetliner, killing all 269 people aboard, an act which prompted President Reagan's accusation that the Soviet Union was "barbaric" and "uncivilized."

When Konstantin Chernenko succeeded Andropov in early 1984, the rhetoric on both sides cooled a bit at first. Chernenko held out hopes for a disarmament agreement if the U.S. would agree to a nuclear freeze and renounce the first use of nuclear weapons. President Reagan noted the "positive elements" in the new Soviet leadership, and hoped that the relationship between the two nations would be put "on a more constructive basis." But as the year progressed and more American missiles were deployed in Europe, more Soviet submarines took up positions off the U.S. coasts, and the Soviets withdrew from the Los Angeles Olympic Games, relationships deteriorated again. In the words of a Kremlin spokesman in June of that year, they had reached the lowest level since the end of World War II. With President Reagan's reelection for four more years, prospects for real improvement seemed dim on both sides, even with the meeting between Secretary of State Schultz and Foreign Minister Gromyko in Geneva in January 1985 to discuss a framework for future arms-control talks.

OUR RESPONSIBILITY

The anxiety we feel under the nuclear shadow can be seriously upsetting. Many have chosen to abate it by blaming the Soviet Union. To focus on the Soviet Union as an aggressor to be deterred frees us from examining the full dynamics of the arms race. Since such an examination would call into question actions of our own country as well, many of us prefer not to embark on that project. Rather than go through a disturbing reevaluation, many become complacent in hostility, resigned to the promise of annihilation to save us from the prospect of domination.

But the promise of annihilation, otherwise known as the doctrine of deterrence, is morally bankrupt. The bishops'

1983 peace pastoral, *The Challenge of Peace*, judged that nuclear deterrence would be a morally acceptable policy only if it did not include plans for protracted nuclear war or a quest for nuclear superiority, and if deterrence is used as a step toward progressive disarmament.[37] In fact, these conditions do not exist. Our government does have plans for protracted nuclear war. It constantly orders new weapons in an ongoing race for superiority. And it enshrines deterrence as the "fundamental goal," in Secretary Schultz's words, of American policy.[38]

To all who have said a resounding "no" to the promise of annihilation embodied in the present policy of nuclear deterrence, who have seen it, as writer Jonathan Schell did, as "something to rebel against,"[39] the reevaluation of our own nation's actions is necessary. After we go through it, we as citizens of one of the two superpowers responsible for the nuclear shadow, can take those democratic steps we have available to change things for the better.

DISCUSSION QUESTIONS

1. The family of a civilian killed when his helicopter was shot down in Nicaragua said he had gone down there "to fight Communism." How pervasive today is the belief that Communism is our enemy?

2. How can we look at Communism from the perspective of the Peace Myth?

3. If investigating the devil turns up as much information about believers' fears and fantasies as about the power of evil itself, what does investigating the Soviet Union reveal about Americans' fears and fantasies?

4. What intentions do you speculate Soviet leaders had in invading Afghanistan? In sending military equipment to Nicaragua?

5. If our real enemies are those on both sides of the international divide who operate the international nuclear weapons system, how can we begin to understand, focus, and negotiate with them?

EPILOGUE

The real threat in the nuclear age is not any single nation, no matter how powerful its arsenal or how strident its rhetoric. The real threat is the international nuclear weapons system in which the danger of extinction is lodged. This system poses a more severe hazard to the human race than any one nation.

The system is a collection of factors which produce the weapons and place them in positions to wreak their havoc. These factors include first the international policies of the superpowers, each holding tenaciously to its own sovereignty and ambitions, each wanting its own way in the world and competing with the other for power and prestige.

They include also the technology responsible for the weapons, technology pushed by state-of-the-art research imperatives, laser breakthroughs, star wars capabilities. If the people in Research and Development say a certain weapon is feasible, regardless of whether or not it serves any identifiable military need, then it is built—to keep ahead of the other side.

A third major factor is the intricate international economy dependent on securing the materials and employing the workers fabricating the war machines. The economy of the United States, and therefore most of Europe and Latin

America, would collapse if weapons production were suddenly stopped.

Reality today, since reality is based on continued existence, demands that the international nuclear weapons system which threatens the extinction of the human race be changed. The system itself has many positive features—justifiable pride in national achievements, imaginative engineering feats, higher standards of living. The system need not be destroyed, but it must be transformed. This means moving from national independence to international interdependence. It means yielding sovereignty in the interests of community. It means turning technology away from meeting weapons needs and toward meeting human needs.

The transformation can only be accomplished by people presently involved in the system—government officials, military personnel, researchers, designers, financiers, industrial workers. It cannot be imposed from outside, because nothing outside the system is powerful enough to turn it around. This means for most of us the hard, persevering effort of reaching out to people who speak a different language, respect a different historical tradition, profess a different philosophy of life, follow a different myth—on whichever side of the international divide they live.

Our immediate need, in fidelity to Jesus' spirit, is to love all those human beings who, because they operate the international nuclear weapons system, are our real enemies. We have to shoulder the burden of understanding, focusing and negotiating with them. Our ultimate goal is to unite with them in facing our common danger.

The challenge is Herculean. Its dimensions are staggering. The effort is burdensome, its countercultural course strewn with obstacles. Then we remember Jesus' promise two millenia ago: "Surely I will be with you always, to the very end of the age" (Matthew 28:20). Because of this promise we share the confidence of Paul when he wrote, "I can do everything through him who gives me strength" (Philippians 4:13).

Everything, even love our enemies.

Everything, even join with them as friends to renew the face of our common home, our earth.

NOTES

CHAPTER ONE

1. Carl Gustav Jung, *The Undiscovered Self* (New York: New American Library, 1958), 114.
2. Thomas Merton, "The Root of War is Fear," *New Seeds of Contemplation* (Norfolk, Connecticut: New Directions, 1961), 113.
3. Robert Coles, "Psychology and Armageddon," *Psychology Today* (May, 1982), 14.
4. Israel W. Charny, *How Can We Commit the Unthinkable?* (Boulder, Colorado: Westview Press, 1982), 186.
5. President Nixon made this remark at a press conference on May 8, 1970, quoted in *Atrocities in Vietnam: Myths and Realities*, by Edward S. Herman (Philadelphia and Boston: Pilgrim Press, 1970), 1.
6. Mary Kay Blakely, "The New Bedford Gang Rape: Who Were the Men?" *MS* magazine (July, 1983), 53.
7. Erich Fromm, *The Anatomy of Human Destructiveness* (New York: Holt, Rinehart and Winston, 1973), 274-5.
8. UPI News story, "Remorseless Nazi Awaits Sentencing," *The Commercial Appeal*, Memphis (July 16, 1983), A-4.
9. "Notes and Comments," *The New Yorker* (February 2, 1976), 25.
10. For an analysis of Group Narcissism, see Fromm, *The Anatomy of Human Destructiveness*, 203-205.
11. J. William Fulbright, "In Thrall to Fear," *The New Yorker* (January 8, 1972), 43.
12. Transcript of the 1982 PBS television program, "George Kennan, a Critical Voice" (New York: Blackwood Production), 15-16.
13. Richard J. Barnet, *Roots of War, the Men and Institutions Behind U.S. Foreign Policy* (Baltimore: Penguin Books, 1972), 115.
14. Kenneth N. Waltz, *Man, the State and War* (New York: Columbia University Press, 1954), 82.
15. Fromm, *The Anatomy of Human Destructiveness*, 207.
16. Charny, *How Can We Commit the Unthinkable?* 123-4.
17. Speech by Joe Henry Eagle, Representative from Texas, in *The Congressional Record*, April 5, 1917, reprinted in *The First World War*, by Jere Clemens King, editor (New York: Harper and Row, 1972), 281.
18. Quoted by Robert Jay Lifton in his article, "The 'Gook Syndrome' and 'Numbered Warfare,'" *Saturday Review* (December, 1972), reprinted in *Peacemaking; a Guide to Conflict Resolution for Individuals, Groups and Nations*, by Barbara Stanford, editor (New York: Bantam Books, 1976), 239.

19. For a description of the accusation that witches were in league with the devil, see Henry Ansgar Kelly, *The Devil, Demonology and Witchcraft*, (Garden City: Doubleday, 1968), chapter three, "Demonic Witchcraft." The numbers of women killed as witches in Europe from the 14th to the 18th century are variously estimated. Richard Woods, O.P., gives a figure of 300,000 in *The Occult Revolution* (New York: Herder and Herder, 1971), 96. William Warren Sweet suggests 500,000 in *The Story of Religion in America* (New York: Harper and Brothers, 1930), 61.

20. From an offical briefing to CIA agents in training, quoted by Ralph W. McGehee, *Deadly Deceits*, (New York: Sheridan Square Publications, 1983), 9-10.

21. Barnet, *Roots of War*, 14.

22. Hannah Arendt, *Eichman in Jerusalem: A Report on the Banality of Evil* (New York: Viking Press, 1965), 85.

CHAPTER TWO

1. Peter Berger has summarized his theory of the sociology of knowledge in the first part of his book *A Rumor of Angels: Modern Society and the Rediscovery of the Supernatural* (Garden City: Anchor Books, 1970), 6.

2. Chandogya Upanishad, IV, 2, 1-4. This excerpt is found in Mircea Eliade, *From Primitives to Zen* (New York: Harper and Row, 1967), 114.

3. Quoted by William James in his essay, "The Moral Equivalent of War." Reprinted in *War and Morality*, Richard A. Wasserstrom, editor (Belmont, California: Wadsworth, 1970), 5.

4. See, for example, Roland de Vaux, *Ancient Israel* (New York: McGraw-Hill, 1961), 258,260.

5. Quoted by John Ferguson, *The Politics of Love* (Cambridge: James Clarke Publishers, n.d.), 103.

6. Quoted by Roland Bainton, *Christian Attitudes Toward War and Peace* (Nashville: Abington, 1960), 111-112.

7. Saint Bernard, "Sermon on the Knights of the Temple," in *War and the Christian Conscience*, by Albert Marrin, editor (Chicago: Henry Regnery, 1971), 82.

8. Quoted by Bainton, *Christian Attitudes Toward War and Peace*, 112-113.

9. St. Thomas Aquinas, *Summa Theologica*, II-II, q. 10, art. 8 (New York: Benziger Brothers, 1947), 1219.

10. Quoted by Roland Bainton, *Christian Attitudes Toward War and Peace*, 168.

11. Quoted by Dorothy Dohen, *Nationalism and American Catholicism* (New York: Sheed and Ward, 1967), 18.

12. Quoted by Joyce Hollyday, "The Battle for Central America," *So-journers* (April, 1982), 20.
13. Quoted by Sydney E. Ahlstrom, *A Religious History of the American People* (Garden City: Image Books, 1975), Volume 2, 367.
14. This version of Deuteronomy is the Jerusalem Bible Translation. All other Scripture quotes in this book, with one exception, are taken from *The Holy Bible, The New International Version* (Grand Rapids: Zondervan Bible Publishers, 1978). The exception is identified in a footnote.
15. Quoted by John Noss, *Man's Religions*, 7th edition (New York: Macmillan, 1984), 250.
16. Swami Prabhavananda and Christopher Isherwood, translators, *The Song of God: Bhagavad-Gita* (New York: Mentor, 1954), 90.
17. *The Challenge of Peace: God's Promise and Our Response*, A letter on War and Peace (Washington, D.C.: National Conference of Catholic Bishops, May 3, 1983), paragraph #73.
18. Edward Schillebeeckx, O.P., "In Search of the Salvific Value of a Political Praxis of Peace," in *Peace Spirituality for Peacemakers* (Antwerp, Belgium: Omega 1983), 37. (Available from Pax Christi, USA).
19. Hans Kung, *On Being a Christian* (New York: Wallaby, 1978), 251.
20. See, for example, Joseph Campbell, "Mythologies of War and Peace," in *Myths to Live By* (New York: Bantam, 1972), 174: "Plainly and simply: it has been the nations, tribes, and people bred to mythologies of war that have survived to communicate their life—supporting mythic lore to descendants."
21. Ashley Montagu, "The New Litany of 'Innate Depravity,' or Original Sin Revisited," in *Man and Aggression*, second edition, Ashley Montagu, editor (London: Oxford University Press, 1973), 16.
22. Charney, *How Can We Commit the Unthinkable?*, 47.
23. *The Challenge of Peace*, paragraph #4.

CHAPTER THREE

1. For a more complete description of the Roman Empire, its extent and its methods, see J.P.V.D. Baldsdon, *Rome: The Story of an Empire* (New York: McGraw-Hill, World University Library, 1970).
2. Gerard S. Sloyan, *Jesus in Focus: A Life in Its Setting* (Mystic, Conn.: Twenty-Third Publications, 1983), 13.
3. John L. McKenzie, *Dictionary of the Bible* (Milwaukee: Bruce, 1965), 668.
4. Rev. Albert Kirk and Robert E. Obach, *A Commentary on the Gospel of Matthew* (New York: Paulist Press, 1978), 230-231.
5. Sloyan, *Jesus in Focus*, 25.
6. Besides Mark 3:6, cf. Mark 12:13 and Matthew 22:16.
7. Leo Trepp, *Judaism: Development and Life* (Encino, California: Dickenson, 1974), 36-37.

8. Cf. Carol Stuhlmueller, C.P., "The Gospel According to Luke," in *The Jerome Biblical Commentary* (Englewood Cliffs, N.J.: Prentice-Hall, 1968), 44:38.
9. Quoted by Eduard Lohse, *The New Testament Environment,* translator John E. Steely, (Nashville: Abingdon, 1976), p. 42.
10. Persecution of Jews by Christians is well known in Jewish circles. For a thorough, sober, and moving study of it by a Catholic priest, see Edward H. Flannery, *The Anguish of the Jews: Twenty-Three Centuries of Anti-Semitism* (New York: Macmillan, 1965).
11. This translation is from the *Revised Standard Version* of the Bible.

CHAPTER FOUR

1. John Piper, *Love Your Enemies* (New York: Cambridge University Press, 1980), 129.
2. Sarah Corson, "Welcoming the Enemy," *Sojourners* (April, 1983), 30-31.
3. Carl R. Rogers, "A Psychologist Looks at Nuclear War," *Journal of Humanistic Psychology,* Vol. 22, No. 4 (Fall, 1982), 13.
4. Roger Fisher, "Fractionating Conflict," in *Conflict Resolution: Contributions of the Behavioral Sciences,* Clagett G. Smith, editor (Notre Dame: University of Notre Dame Press, 1971), 161.
5. Martin Luther King, Jr., *Strength to Love* (New York: Pocket Books, 1964), 42.
6. Martin Luther King, Jr., *Why We Can't Wait* (New York: Mentor Books), 79.
7. Gene Sharp, *The Politics of Nonviolent Action* (Boston: Porter Sargent, 1973), 470.
8. Sharp, *The Politics of Nonviolent Action,* 89-90.
9. Dorothy T. Samuel, *Safe Passage on City Streets* (Nashville: Abingdon, 1975), 13-17.
10. Roger Fisher and William Ury, *Getting to Yes: Negotiating Agreement Without Giving In* (New York: Penguin Books, 1983), 25.
11. Karen Malpede, "A Talk for the Conference on Feminism and Militarism," in *Reweaving the Web of Life: Feminism and Nonviolence,* Pam McAllister, editor (Philadelphia: New Society, 1982), 204.
12. Charny, *How Can We Commit the Unthinkable?,* 95.
13. Erich Fromm, *The Art of Loving* (New York: Bantam Books), 98.
14. Samuel, *Safe Passage on City Streets,* 89.
15. Mahatma Gandhi, *All Men Are Brothers* (New York: Continuum, 1980), 83.
16. Mohandas K. Gandhi, *Non-Violent Resistance* (New York: Schocken, 1961), 46.
17. Samuel, *Safe Passage on City Streets,* 65-66.
18. Quoted in Charny, *How Can We Commit The Unthinkable?,* 251.

19. Bob Hutchinson, "Christians in an Immoral World," *America* (January 28, 1984), 52.
20. *The Challenge of Peace*, paragraph #225.
21. Ibid., #257.
22. Ibid., #73.
23. Ibid., #80.
24. Ibid., #78.

CHAPTER FIVE

1. Quoted in Barnet, *Roots of War*, 19.
2. United States Senate, *Final Report of The Select Committee to Study Governmental Operations With Respect to Intelligence Activities*, Book I (Washington, D.C.: U.S. Government Printing Office, 1976), 19 and 22.
3. John F. McManus, "What About Nuclear Madness?" in *The John Birch Society Bulletin* (May, 1982), article reprint, 4.
4. William F. Buckley, column published in *The Commercial Appeal* (Memphis, November 1, 1983), A-4.
5. Douglas Waitley, *The War Makers* (Washington, D.C.: Robert B. Luce, 1971), 178.
6. Andrei Gromyko, *Press Conference* (Moscow: Novosti Press Agency Publishing House, 1983).
7. Senate Intelligence Committee Report, 268.
8. Quoted in Robert G. Kaiser, *Russia: The People and The Powers* (New York: Atheneum, 1976), 458.
9. Quoted in Robert Scheer, *With Enough Shovels: Reagan, Bush and Nuclear War* (New York, Random House, 1982), 48-49.
10. Address before the Regional Foreign Policy Conference, Birmingham, Alabama, March 22, 1984. Published by the U.S. Department of State, Bureau of Public Affairs, Current Policy No. 558.
11. Morris A. Bealle, *Red Rat Race* (Washington, D.C.: Columbia Publishing Co., 1953), 7.
12. Kaiser, *Russia*, 451.
13. Kaiser, *Russia*, 21-22.
14. George Konrad, "A Path Toward Peace," in *The Atlantic Monthly* (March, 1984), 74.
15. Samuel Moore translator, *The Communist Manifesto* (Chicago: Great Books Foundation, 1955).
16. Selections from "State and Revolution," by V.I. Lenin, in *Readings In World Politics*, second edition, by Robert A. Goldwin, editor (New York: Oxford University Press, 1970), 282.
17. Strobe Talbott, translator and editor, *Khrushchev Remembers: The Last Testament* (Boston: Little, Brown and Company, 1974), 301.

18. 1977 Constitution of the Soviet Union, art. 52. Quoted by Owen Hardwicke, "Faith and Peace in the Soviet Union," in *Just Peace: Journal of Pax Christi* (London: Pax Christi England, 1984).
19. Quoted by Danny Collum in "Anti-Communism: Our State Religion," *Sojourners* (November, 1982), 19.
20. Quoted in the Ground Zero book *What About the Russians—And Nuclear War?* (New York: Pocket Books, 1983), 114.
21. J. N. Westwood, *Russia Since 1917* (New York: St. Martin's Press, 1980), 102.
22. Graham Lyons, editor, *The Russian Version of The Second World War?* (New York: Facts on File Publications, 1976), 12.
23. John Toland, *The Rising Sun: The Decline and Fall of the Japanese Empire* (New York: Bantam Books, 1970), 869.
24. Lyons, *The Russian Version of the Second World War*, 86.
25. Quoted in Fulbright, "In Thrall to Fear," 41.
26. Senate Intelligence Committee Report, 105.
27. Quoted in Gregg Herken, *The Winning Weapon: The Atomic Bomb in The Cold War 1945-1950* (New York: Alfred A. Knopf, 1980), 269.
28. Senate Intelligence Committee Report, 9.
29. Fulbright, "In Thrall to Fear," 42.
30. Senate Intelligence Committee Report, 51.
31. Quoted in Herbert L. Matthews, *Revolution in Cuba: An Essay in Understanding* (New York: Charles Scribner's Sons, 1975), 153.
32. Quoted in Walter LaFeber, "Inevitable Revolutions," *The Atlantic Monthly* (June, 1982), 75.
33. Matthews, *Revolution in Cuba*, 165.
34. Talbott, *Khrushchev Remembers*, 53.
35. Quoted in Lynn Montross, *War Through The Ages* revised edition (New York: Harper and Row, 1960), 996.
36. Talbott, *Khrushchev Remembers*, 444.
37. *The Challenge of Peace*, paragraph #188.
38. Address to the Senate Armed Services Committee, April 20, 1983. Published by the U.S. Department of State, Bureau of Public Affairs, Current Policy No. 480. For an analysis of U.S. defense policy in light of the bishops' Pastoral, see "The Challenge of Peace, Its Promise and Impact: An Assessment," by the National Council of Pax Christi USA, October, 1984.
39. Jonathan Schell, *The Fate of The Earth* (New York: Alfred A. Knopf, 1982), 184.

BASIC RESOURCES

Barnet, Richard J. *Roots of War: The Men and Institutions Behind U.S. Foreign Policy.* Baltimore: Penguin Books, 1972.

Campbell, Joseph. *Myths to Live By.* New York: Bantam Books, 1972.

Charny, Israel W. *How Can We Commit the Unthinkable?* Boulder: Westview, 1982.

Ferguson, John. *The Politics of Love.* Cambridge, England: James Clarke Publishers, n.d.

Fisher, Roger, and William Ury. *Getting to Yes: Negotiating Agreement Without Giving In.* New York: Penguin Books, 1983.

Fromm, Erich. *The Anatomy of Human Destructiveness.* New York: Holt, Rinehart and Winston, 1973.

Gandhi, Mohandas K. *Non-Violent Resistance.* New York: Schocken, 1961.

Juergensmeyer, Mark. *Fighting with Gandhi: A Step-by-Step Strategy for Resolving Everyday Conflicts.* San Francisco: Harper and Row, 1984.

Jung, Carl Gustav. *The Undiscovered Self.* New York: New American Library, 1958.

Kaiser, Robert G. *Russia: The People and the Powers.* New York: Atheneum, 1976.

King, Martin Luther, Jr. *Strength to Love.* New York: Pocket Books, 1964.

Khrushchev Remembers: The Last Testament, translated and edited by Strobe Talbott. Boston: Little, Brown, 1974.

Lyons, Graham, ed. *The Russian Version of the Second World War.* New York: Facts on File Publications, 1976.

Matthews, Herbert L. *Revolution in Cuba: An Essay in Understanding.* New York: Charles Scribner's Sons, 1975.

Merton, Thomas. *New Seeds of Contemplation.* Norfolk, Conn.; New Directions, 1961.

Pastoral Letter on War and Peace, *The Challenge of Peace: God's Promise and Our Response.* Washington: National Conference of Catholic Bishops, 1983.

Piper, John. *Love Your Enemies.* New York: Cambridge University Press, 1980.

Samuel, Dorothy T. *Safe Passage on City Streets.* Nashville: Abingdon, 1975.

Sharp, Gene. *The Politics of Nonviolent Action.* Boston: Porter Sargent Publishers, 1973.

Shipler, David K. *Russia: Broken Idols, Solemn Dreams.* New York: Times Books, 1983.

Sloyan, Gerard S. *Jesus in Focus: A Life in Its Setting.* Mystic, Conn.: Twenty-Third Publications, 1983.

Vanderhaar, Gerard A. *Christians and Nonviolence in the Nuclear Age.* Mystic, Conn.: Twenty-Third Publications, 1982.

_____. *Nonviolence in Christian Tradition.* London, England: Pax Christi, 1982. (Available from Pax Christi USA: 348 E. 10th St., Erie, PA 16503)

Waitley, Douglas. *The War Makers.* Washington: Robert B. Luce, 1971.

Westwood, J.N. *Russia Since 1917.* New York: St. Martin's Press, 1980.